Tangible Traces

Dutch Architecture and Design in the making

Tangible Traces

Dutch Architecture
and Design in the making

NAi Publishers

Contents

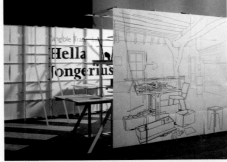

The walls are white, the tables are white, the chairs are white – bare white and thereby stripped of any reference, as if the space has no present or past and is ready to receive the future, what is new. And that is exactly what happens in the exhibition *Tangible Traces*, which began in 2007 as the Dutch contribution to the 7th São Paulo International Architecture Biennial and, after having travelled to Austria, Hong Kong and Indonesia, is being presented in the Netherlands in 2009. Work by one of the participants has been positioned in front of each of the five walls. The *Cinema for two persons* by spatial designer Frank Havermans, the *Polder Sofa* by the industrial designer Hella Jongerius, a felt fabric by textile designer Claudy Jongstra, scale models by the architecture office Onix, and clothing ensembles by the fashion designer Alexander van Slobbe thus literally confer form and colour on the empty space, leaving tangible traces behind.

Various interventions have been effected to make the world behind the result visible too. Each wall contains a life-sized black-and-white drawing of the studio of the designer in question. This glance behind the scenes radiates a level of abstraction and bareness that are in sharp contrast with the reality and aesthetics of the objects on show. Behind each wall there is also a small table with a specially produced book on the work of the designer concerned. It provides insight into the process which underlies the creation of these objects. The background information has therefore become part of the exhibition itself.

Industrial designer Jurgen Bey has based the structure and context of his exhibition design on Modernism. *Tangible Traces* makes use of Modernist features such as the colour white and the idea of the space as a tabula rasa to provide a commentary. After all, the designers presented here do not regard everlasting innovation, the trademark of Modernism, as the highest good. They do not want to start with an empty page. They find tradition and context important and incorporate traces of it in their work.

Hella Jongerius is a perfect example of this. Almost all her designs are characterised by a reinterpretation of existing forms and patterns. For instance, in several commissions by Koninklijke Tichelaar Makkum, the oldest ceramics factory in the Netherlands, she gave her own twist to the traditional Delft Blue decorations. She also made classical-looking vases from rubber, an unusual, soft material. Moreover, she created a history in her own oeuvre with different editions of these *Soft Urns* (the colour of medieval glass in 1994, pink in 1999). Frank Havermans and Onix do the same in architecture by deliberately responding to the setting, that is, to the kind of landscape, the visual axes and the buildings that are already present, or to the history that lies concealed there. Local features are incorporated in the design and the architects elaborate upon a generally recognisable language of forms. *Multifunctional Shed* (1999) by Onix, for example, is based on the archetype of a shed, a form that everybody will be able to recognise, without necessarily coming from a particular region. The treehouse *KAPKAR / ZZW-220* (2006) by Frank Havermans is orientated towards the trees in the surroundings that have all grown facing in the same direction because of the harsh onshore wind. The outside of this place to sleep looks like the sheds in the region: black with a white frame around the door, so that they are still clearly visible at night by the light of the moon.

The designers in *Tangible Traces* are representatives of an attitude towards design that has been around in the Netherlands for some time, but has never been so clearly named and shown before. For years they have been working, partly out of the limelight, on an oeuvre in which they formulate an intelligent response to new conditions such as globalisation, standardisation and commercialisation. Quality is what matters to them and in order to achieve this, they cherish their autonomy and want to operate independently. So they determine on personal grounds exactly what they reuse from the physical surroundings and their history. Deeper layers of meaning are penetrated through a new attention to detail, context and the local, the rediscovery of forgotten handicraft techniques, and through a fascination with ordinary materials and archetypes. Their level of integrity is extremely high and this is precisely why their call for less innovation for innovation's sake and for more commitment has remained so implicit and has therefore not achieved recognition. *Tangible Traces* shows, thanks to them, that Dutch architecture, design and fashion have gradually become less typically Dutch precisely by becoming more rooted in the traditions of the Netherlands.

More commitment

'Typically Dutch' – 'SuperDutch' in architecture – is a qualification that has been in use since the 1990s. It stands for the conceptual approach of Dutch architects and designers who stand an excellent chance abroad. With the architect Rem Koolhaas at the prow, and Droog Design and the fashion duo Viktor & Rolf in his wake, these designers comment on their profession and the world. The commentary is contained in the work itself. Sloping rooms and folded floors make fun of the logic of building structures. A tablecloth with an amalgamated bowl reinvents 'the regular table arrangement'. What a new perfume smells like is a guessing game when it is launched on the market solely as campaign, as representation. In short: a conceptual attitude towards design means raising questions about the demand or the assignment. For these designers the design process is often considered more important than the product. What count are the underlying ideas and the game. An ironical, light-hearted, experimental, provocative and pragmatic view of reality, as well as a traditional Dutch preference for simplicity, are what link these designers.

The architects and designers of *Tangible Traces* were at work during the same period. Apart from Hella Jongerius

and Alexander van Slobbe, who were considered to belong to the conceptual current, they got on with the job on their own and without attracting too much notice. This was not only because the often raw and outspoken work of their colleagues attracted all the attention, but also because at the time there was simply not enough support for their ideas. They also work conceptually and favour sobriety, it is true, but the main difference is that for them the concept is not the end. The final product, the result of the creative process, is more important.

The tide began to turn around the time of the opening of *Reality Machines. Het alledaagse weerspiegeld in hedendaagse Nederlandse architectuur, fotografie en vormgeving* [Mirroring the Everday in Contemporary Dutch Architecture, Photography and Design], the exhibition on more than ten years of conceptual thought and design that the NAI presented in 2003. Much conceptual work suffered from erosion and had degenerated to the level of a feeble joke. A modest process of reflection got under way. Critics targeted the flippancy of conceptualism and called for more ideological and critical standpoints. The professional journals called for reflection and meditation on professional practice. There was talk of a 'new engagement', although opinions were divided on what it precisely was. At any rate, it was no politically or ideologically motivated engagement, but a great diversity in 'commitment to social problems and to the determination of the position of the architect, the artist and the designer', as Simon Franke, the director of NAi Publishers, put it at the time (*Reflect #01: New Commitment. In architecture, art and design*, 2003). At the same time, the demand for functionality also slowly made a comeback. The demand arose for items of furniture like the *Polder Sofa* (2005), which Jongerius designed as a commission for the Swiss Vitra: a beautiful, high-quality sofa that is first and foremost comfortable to sit in, and not just a parody of the idea of a couch.

The U-turn is perhaps the most obvious in architecture.

While the Netherlands had for a long time been the Walhalla for young architects, after the economic recession that followed on the heels of the terrorist attack of 11 September 2001, the commissions were placed again with the established names like Mecanoo, Jo Coenen and Herman Hertzberger. In addition there were the architects with star allure such as Frank O. Gehry, Zaha Hadid and Daniel Libeskind, who were welcomed and deployed all over the world to clean up the image of a city with architectural icons in an act of city branding. Dissatisfaction with these developments grew. Onix, which had been established in 1994 but had never joined the conceptual current that was popular at the time, even wrote several manifestos. According to the firm, they did so in the first instance for themselves 'in order to understand and position their own work'. One of the ten rules in *DogmA* (2001), inspired by the Danish film association Dogma 1995, was: 'The architect must not be credited'. The 2005 manifesto was called *Awaiting Signification. MaNUfesto for an authentic experience of architecture*. That too appealed to the desire for a broader perspective, for more commitment to one's own work, to one's own profession, to society.

The desire for more meaning and depth is also characteristic of the other designers in *Tangible Traces*. And that is not so strange in a world where uniformity is the rule rather than the exception as the result of mass production and internet communication. However, they convert the grand words and aims of the worldwide movement of anti-globalists or alternative globalists into something very pragmatic, realistic, and often on a very small scale. In connection with the presentation of the AM NAI Prize for architects below the age of forty, the critic Lara Schrijver wrote in *Bare Facts* (2006) as follows: 'Perhaps the greatest strength of this group of architects is that they continue to work on their ideal world, which at the same time is not as rigorously laid down as in the ideologies of earlier generations (...) Let this be their strength: they understand that a utopia is unattainable, that you can only fail, but that in the meantime you can still make something beautiful now and then'. The committed designers do not have the intention of saving the world and they also continue to strive for aesthetic objectives with their designs. The least and the most that they can do is to assume responsibility for what they make themselves in relation to their own discipline. Their motivation is quality, a criterion which is open to discussion, but that here at any rate coincides with a critical and self-aware attitude to work. This attitude to work, which can manifest itself in a variety of ways, is what *Tangible Traces* is about.

More attention

Some textiles are so rough that they seem almost fresh from the sheep. Others make you want to stroke them or have a refined glitter; they may be in natural beige or flaming red. Claudy Jongstra's works in felt are the result of an extremely discriminating and controlled way of working. She has an encyclopaedic knowledge of the properties and qualities of innumerable types of wool. She knows how to use the material pure or in combination with silk or metal, for example. The felt-making process itself, in which the wool is moistened so that the scales stand upright and interlock, is an aleatory art with which she is so familiar by now that she can programme the result. With her own flock of Drenthe moorland sheep (a protected species) and a Dutch plant garden that she has created herself, she has full control of the entire production process from shepherding to dyeing.

If anything characterises the attitude to work of Claudy Jongstra and those who think like her, it is the attention to construction down to the tiniest details. How something is made and fits together is so important that it remains visible in the result. This extreme focus on the work itself can also be clearly seen in the buildings designed by Frank Havermans and Onix. Havermans' obsession with

technique even goes to such extremes that he makes his objects without drawings, purely on the basis of a perfectly elaborated scale model. He also builds everything by hand, all by himself.

Closely linked to this focus on the tactile product is the return of craftsmanlike techniques. For instance, Onix leaves room in the building process for the skilled knowledge of local builders and restoration sub-contractors. Alexander van Slobbe's clothes are characterised by a large variety of details – ruffs, borders, buttons, beads – that are pile-woven, knitted, woven, embroidered, crocheted, punched or dyed by hand, often using techniques from the past. He also makes use of moulage, the oldest technique for making clothes and patterns, in which the ideal shape is found by wrapping fabric around a body or tailor's dummy. This fresh appreciation of craftsmanship is part of an international tendency. The 2003 publication *The Future is Handmade* by the Prince Claus Fund dealt not only with historical applied arts, but also with the

role that craft plays by now in the work of countless contemporary artists and designers. Craftsmanship implies paying attention to what is local, but while handmade products were traditionally used as an expression of a local group identity, nowadays they are also being deployed to address a larger world. That is possible, the artist and writer Louise Schouwenberg claims, because handiwork is free of the negative connotations of regression, nostalgia and bourgeois values. Thanks to the process of industrialisation, renewal has proceeded at such a pace

that such notions as 'old' and 'new' have become relative. Craftsmanlike techniques and motifs have been incorporated in new discourses, new media, new processes of production, new distribution channels, and new social contexts.

With its ups and downs, the fresh appreciation of what is local has been the topic of discussion in fashion and architecture for some time. Japanese fashion designers

introduced traditional techniques of treating fabrics in the 1980s. Famous examples are the jumper with holes by Comme des Garçons (the lack of a definitive form is a typically Japanese design principle) and the *Pleats Please* line by Issey Miyake, based on the traditional Japanese technique of pleating. By now designers all over the world are reacting to the phenomena of provenance and tradition, as the Fashion Weeks that have appeared everywhere in the last decade and which focus primarily on their own local culture clearly show. For the exhibition *Gejaagd door de Wind* [Gone with the wind], which recently opened in the Zuiderzeemuseum in Enkhuizen, the guest curators Francisco van Benthum and Alexander van Slobbe invited more than forty designers, photographers and stylists to come up with a contemporary design based on typical Dutch traditional clothing. According to Alexander van Slobbe, an exhibition like that would have been unthinkable twenty years ago. He even claims: 'It is necessary to call yourself Dutch in order to face up to the foreign competition'.

The local element in the form of attention to the region has gained increasing ground in architecture in the last few years. Operating from the local context has become generally accepted in architecture and urban planning since the 1980s in reaction to the *tabula rasa* and anonymity of Modernism. The reappraisal of the local element in the 1980s was given a warm reception internationally through the critical regionalism that was launched by Alexander Tzonis and Liane Lefaivre and achieved worldwide recognition through Kenneth Frampton's essay *Towards a Critical Regionalism. Six Points for an Architecture of Resistance* (1983). Regionalism is a deliberate search to unify the local with the global, the conservative with the innovative, and to identify the specificity of a location (topography, climate, architectural traditions) without lapsing into the mere imitation of existing local architectural typologies. For a long time this architectural search was played out primarily at the level of discussion and the formation of theory. The issue becomes clearly visible, however, in the design practice of Onix: the attention for the local situation remains a free interpretation of the setting, so that there is always a tension between the result and what is directly recognisable.

The catalogue *Global Fashion Local Tradition* (2005, Centraal Museum/Artez) suggests a range of possible explanations for latching on to one's own or to other people's traditions. The preservation of traditions of local history is often regarded as a reaction to globalisation. In that case craftsmanship is a way of regaining a certain unique cultural identity in a world in which everything is growing more and more uniform. Arts and crafts 'to touch base and to feel real matter in an ever more complex information-laden society', as the design expert Li Edelkoort formulates it. However, it can also be a political comment on the hegemony and temporary character of the fashion world of the West. A designer like John Galliano used a variety of handicraft techniques out of pure interest for craftsmanship in the wide sense and saw the global world in that respect as a huge department store that was ideal for shopping. Vivienne Westwood imposed a task on herself: to save craftsmanship from the levelling effects of the prêt-à-porter industry. However that may be, they are motivations that each go beyond the exoticism that has been a source of inspiration and innovation for centuries.

If we look at *Tangible Traces*, it is striking how subtly the five designers use craftsmanship, but also how they maintain a distance in falling back on tradition. If the finding of a local toehold is already a motif, these designers do it in an entirely original way and are at the same time bent on creating something new, in spite of their dislike of the 'new new new motto'. In their case the old and the new combine to create a surplus. Their products are certainly not historicising Dutch and in most cases they also meet with a warm reception abroad. Take Alexander van

Slobbe. He started to use handicrafts primarily to bring tradition back to the Dutch fashion industry and to create a place for the multi-faceted Dutch identity and society. But whether he has his pearls à la Vermeer fired by Royal Tichelaar, introduces hand-woven labels in Dutch manufactured products, or incorporates antique Turkish embroidery, his clothes as a whole are not a bit less sober or contemporary as a result, and the dry, so-called abstract Dutch style is not lost either.

It is precisely because of their subtle approach that working with attention and aiming at quality seem to be the main motives of the designers in *Tangible Traces*. They find that attention and aiming at quality in working in a craftsmanlike way, which is why they welcome the handicraft techniques. In this they differ from Marlies Dekkers, for example, who produced a one-off collection of Delft Blue lingerie in 2007 and opened her store in Paris with models with white caps on a Delft Blue carpet, or from Viktor & Rolf, who surprised the public at around the same time with a fashion show inspired by Dutch costume, in which the models walked on clogs. Those actions look above all like attempts to poke fun at the foreign cliché of the Netherlands, or perhaps their butt is even the flirt of the international fashion world with everything that is local.

More personality

He has chosen the wooden planks from the DIY shop or from the demolition site himself for the knots in the wood. The material may be cheap, but the care with which it is selected and the patterns that those knots combine to form have an evident added value. In fact, what has become the studio apartment in a guest atelier of Frank Havermans near Vught has become unique because of it.

Striving for uniqueness in your work is another way to distinguish yourself and to give meaning to a globalising

world. All of the designers in *Tangible Traces* employ a way of working that is geared to expressing more personality. The use of improvisation is the most extreme of these resources, which is at odds with both the highly conscientious method of working of craftsmen and the control and uniformity of mechanised production. When Hella Jongerius deliberately has her semi-manufactures fired at too high a temperature, the result is unpredictable forms (*B-set Dinner Service*, 1998). When Onix improves installations on location, like the Estonian bird's nests which can accommodate a complete human family, elements specific to the location are optimised to the full and architecture becomes a product of the present moment – and, of course, no present moment is like any other.

The concept of uniqueness is a tricky one. When is a product really distinctive? The search for a symbiosis, for a new balance between serial production and handicraft techniques, has been a thread running through the work of Hella Jongerius for years. But are not the vases and tapestries that she has made for the Swedish Ikea company in the last few years simply mass products, even if they were produced in a limited edition? Or is it justified to speak of 'a genuine Jongerius' every time because she has given particular attention to the detail of every item in the collection – hand-painted in China or hand-woven in India – so that no exemplar is identical to the others? 'I try to make individuals within families', as she once put it herself.

By extension, the question of uniqueness inevitably raises that of authenticity, a qualification that has been particularly current in the last few years. Is a unique product by definition authentic too? And if so, in what sense and for whom, the designer or the user? Although the word implies a negative judgement, in the context of the reappraisal of what is local and craftsmanlike it has a primarily positive connotation: authentic in the sense of genuine and original. Authenticity is a topic all over the

world, and particularly in most of the countries where *Tangible Traces* has been shown. How do such countries as China, Taiwan, India and Brazil, which are making an enormous economic sprint and are urbanising at an astonishing rate, cope with the extreme quantity of Western input in relation to their own culture? One's own culture can be represented very literally, but one wonders whether there are also designers who, like the participants in *Tangible Traces*, reinterpret more the subtle elements that are not immediately recognisable for an outsider such as spatial relations.

Linked to the question of uniqueness, personality, authenticity or whatever name is given to it are the personal contribution and control of the designer in the creation of the product. These are no longer taken for granted in an era of mass production, and the designers of *Tangible Traces* seem to want to distance themselves from this. Claudy Jongstra has control of the entire process from raw material to product in order to be able to operate independently. Frank Havermans does everything himself and lets the human dimension determine his designs. His contemplative spaces, such as the video room in *Tangible Traces* where the visitor can see how Frank Havermans makes the video room in his workshop, are often only accessible for one or two persons. Alexander van Slobbe deliberately stopped his successful SO line for men and breathed a new lease of life into his earlier Orson + Bodil line for women because he wanted to produce on a small scale again, to have contact with his clients, and to be able to make his clothes himself instead of having to fly all over the world all the time.

The focus on construction and detail, the recourse to laborious handicraft techniques, the use of such sustainable materials as wood and wool, the striving for a distinctive product, the personal attention of the designer: in fact they are all characteristics of what used to be considered luxury. In her book *Deluxe — how luxury lost its luster*

(2007), the US journalist Dana Thomas describes how
the notion of luxury has been given a different content in
the course of time and has lost its status as a hallmark of
quality. Originally it was a matter of quality for the happy
few. Luxury stood for tradition, power, success, superi-
ority, exclusivity. At the end of the nineteenth century
the process of democratisation started that was eventually to reduce luxury primarily to an emotion that is ex-
pressed above all in accessories that are available to all.
After a dip during the political revolution of the 1960s,
the emergence of the unmarried woman manager in the
1980s created a fresh market for luxury. By transferring
production to countries where labour power was cheap-
er, a wider group could be catered for: the middle class.
One-man businesses with hand-made unique items were
transformed overnight into brands with a worldwide re-
tail market.

In reaction to this new luxury market, in which the
'must have handbag' triumphs above all, an alternative movement has got under way in the last few years.
Dana Thomas calls them the luxury refugees: 'designers, perfumers and executives who grew so disillusioned
with the compromises and greed of the luxury corporate world that they fled and started something small and
independent that would allow them to do what drew
them to business in the first place: create the best that
money could buy'. These words could have been written by Alexander van Slobbe, in that they describe exactly
what he has done. In a recent interview with the Dutch
daily NRC Handelsblad on the occasion of his appointment
as director of the Design Academy in Eindhoven and the
opening of his NL=New Luxury shop in Amsterdam, he
remarked that quality has taken on a new meaning for
him: 'Less fast and trendy, with more content and more
thought out'. Luxury will no longer be luxury because of
the label: 'The big expensive brands have claimed luxury
and I want to win it back. The personal touch means

much more than a big marketing budget. The new luxury
is that of the small-scale, hand-made, sustainable'. From
this perspective the endless quest for the right knots in the
wood or the making of felt by hand are also pure luxury,
however inexpensive or basic the wooden planks or curls
of wool may be. As the French shoe designer Christian
Loubatin so beautifully phrased it: 'Luxury is not con-
sumerism. It is educating the eyes to see that special
quality'.

It should be evident that quality is the comprehensive criterion for the designers in *Tangible Traces*. They reinterpret
forms, images and techniques from local traditions, crafts
and existing collections, a method that matches their
sharply focused gaze and attitude. And although a whiff
of nostalgia clings to the projects, they are clearly contemporary through the incorporation of the latest technolo-
gies and an unmistakably Dutch conceptual way of thinking. The designers do not allow the flavour of the week
and the fickleness of the world to get on top of them. In
the food industry you could compare them with slow
food philosophy. And although they do not form a movement, they already appear to have had an impact on many
young designers. Take *Villa 1* by Powerhouse Company,
the architecture office of Nanne de Ru and Charles
Bessard. This house in the woods, inspired by Norwegian
peasant cottages and Mies van der Rohe's Farnsworth
House among other things, is a paragon of architectural
detailing and is a genuine Gesamtkunstwerk. In fashion,
the young designer Mattijs van Bergen made much use of
a certain pleating technique for his graduation collection
at the Central Saint Martin's College of Art and Design in
London in 2008, and in *Gejaagd door de Wind* [Gone with
the wind] he fell back on the fan-shaped folds of traditional costume from the Overijssel region. That design
can be even more basic and modest was shown by Lonny
van Rijswijck, who graduated from the Design Academy

in Eindhoven in 2006 with the project *Uit de klei getrokken* [From the bog]. She made a service of clay that she had collected with her own hands from different parts of the Netherlands. The provenance of the service remains visible because each type of clay has its own colour and structure. 'This contemporary service is an ode to a hand-icraft tradition without lapsing into nostalgic sentiment' was the verdict of the Dutch daily *de Volkskrant*. Of course, you never know whether and for how long the desire for more commitment, more attention and more personality will be able to stand up to the future, but for the present generation of designers quality, craftsmanship and tradition are at any rate no longer old-fashioned words.

Linda Vlassenrood, curator *Tangible Traces*, NAI
Mirjam van der Linden, journalist

Frank Havermans

Frank Havermans

The spatial installations by Frank Havermans (b. 1967) reveal a profound fascination with construction and display the meticulous use of relatively inexpensive types of timber. Havermans structures his projects using basic tools and without calling on builders or structural engineers. He deliberately maintains a great distance from standard architectural practice. He does not make architectural drawings, but designs using nothing more than models. These working models are the spatial and structural research, and therefore serve as proof of a project's structural feasibility. Unusually, the installation is therefore a literal enlargement of the final model. Havermans always builds his installations alone and the human scale is therefore decisive for their design and realization. A high degree of exclusivity is implicit in the protracted development process as well as in the well-considered and honest handling of the material in relation to the construction. The objects are extremely tactile, rugged and elegant at one and the same time. There is invariably an element of quiet repose in the spatial installations by Havermans. This contemplative effect, which is inherent to small spaces, stems from the question of how little space one needs to escape one's surroundings.

Filmed footage of KAPKAR / TT-C2P

"I avoid luxury in the sense of indolence and convenience. Bubble baths, open kitchens, fenced staircases: they strip us of all danger, uncertainty, initiative. They are interventions that make us duller. They do not encourage you to think about what you are doing in that space. Regulations and interference are far-reaching, especially in the Netherlands. Every footpath is flanked by signs and benches; there is no comparison with a mountain path in Norway.

My designs challenge the user to find his or her own solution. They deliberately incorporate inconveniences, such as a door where you have to enter, or a cupboard with a sloping part. The user has to assume personal responsibility. A design does not always have to be useful to you, it can be the other way around. That idea is completely accepted in fashion: how many women walk on uncomfortable shoes with heels that are too high for them? That kind of thing is not allowed in the case of a cupboard. You can look at it this way: I make images that fill the space and can also be used.

A design has to be spatially interesting, constructionally challenging, and made of exciting material. That is what quality means to me. I use 'low-quality' wood from a DIY store or a demolition site; it is not meant for cupboards at all. I find it a beautiful material, it is strong and cheap, although the working, the finishing, takes a lot of time. As an artist, it is normal for me to do everything myself. Besides, I like the physical aspect of architecture, I love material and making things. My designs are so complex and are so close to the material itself – every knot in the wood is important to me – that I do not in fact entrust the work to anyone else. For *Tangible Traces* I have specially made a real building because architecture biennials like the one in São Paulo actually only show representations of buildings. It has become a cinema showing a film about the making of this cinema, because the process of making has such an important place in my work. So the building has been built solely to show itself – which often seems to be the purpose of much present-day architecture as well. The fact that there is only room for two people is because I like to give people a peaceful spot. I like to be by myself."

Projects
1998-2008

Project	architectural installation
Date	10 February - 8 March 1998
Location	De Overslag artists' initiative
	Eindhoven, the Netherlands
Material	structural plywood, timber
	beams, screws, latex

The installation was a replica of the exhibition space on the scale 1:3. The door and window openings of the modelled room were connected with the existing doors and windows using perspectival shafts, allowing the model to float in the room. A balcony overlooking the void offered a view of the model and simultaneously gave access to the installation. The space between the model and the exhibition space could be explored via two door openings on the ground floor.

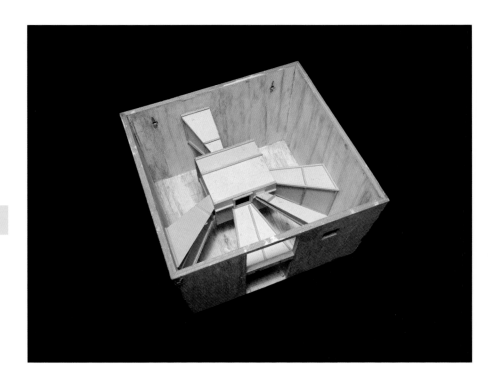

Reception Area / Mail Room

Project   item of furniture / art object
Date   2000
Location   ZIN in Werk
    Vught, the Netherlands
Material   structural plywood, birch multi-
    ply board, timber beams, screws,
    lacquer, latex

The assignment was to design panelling for the reception area with materials recycled from the former monastery. However, Havermans also incorporated the adjacent mail room in his design. He drew inspiration from the building's remaining original windows and copied them on the scale of 1:1. He then rotated the 'windows' by 90 and 180 degrees, and secured them on and into the wall. By adding depth to these 'windows', Havermans has created an item of furniture in the mail room and an art object in the reception area.

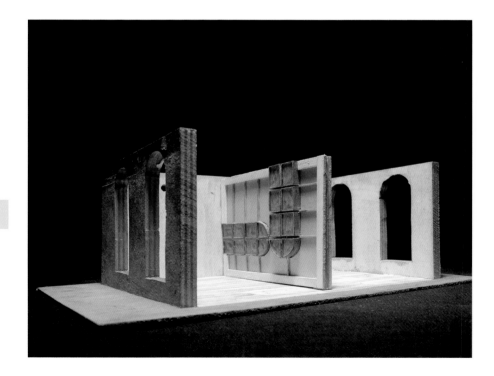

Project	studio apartment in guest atelier
Date	2004
Location	ZIN in Werk
	Vught, the Netherlands
Material	structural plywood, wooden
	beams, glass, polyester, lacquer

On the Huize Steenwijk country estate at the edge of Vught stands the former monastery of the Brothers of Tilburg, which was renovated and extended by Marx & Steketee Architects. The monastery is now used as a centre for meditation run by the ZIN foundation. In the middle of the grounds stands an old barn that serves as an atelier for guest artists. The barn is 15 metres long, 7 metres wide and has a ridge height of 7.5 metres. During renovation, the northern elevation was replaced by a brick wall with five large windows. As the first guest artist, Havermans was asked to make the barn inhabitable for temporary stays. Havermans wanted to leave the roof structure as it was and accentuate it where possible. The living accommodation occupies part of the barn and is a 'free-hanging' structure. The living quarters are composed of different volumes containing a bedroom, living room, bathroom and kitchen. There is one volume that contrarily penetrates through the apex of the gable and has a large window. This volume offers a panoramic view across the estate and the cemetery, serving as a space for contemplation.

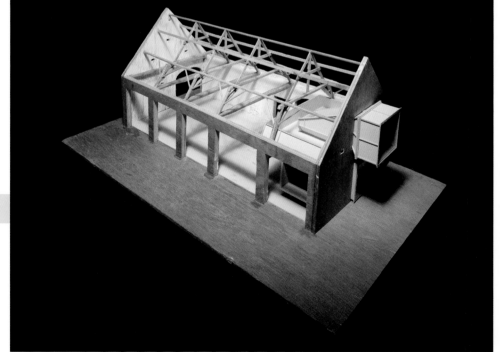

Project	architectural installation
Date	2 October - 27 November 2005
Location	art event 'Mijn Domein', Zware Plaatwerkerij, Koninklijke Schelde Werf, Flushing, the Netherlands
Material	recycled plywood, wooden beams, connectors, bolts, nuts

The industrial hall of the former shipyard has been made accessible by this installation. The façade of this industrial hall functions as a kind of old city wall and divides the world of heavy labour on the shipyard from the world of recreational shopping in the city centre. To bring about a dialogue between the shipyard and the city centre, Havermans has reopened a 30-year-old close-welded and hidden small fire door. This opening has led to the appearance of the architectural construction *KAPKAR / KSV-800* and also forms the entrance. To enter the construction, you have to walk out of the hall through the crowded shopping street and climb the stairs of the construction through the small fire door. In the control cabin on top, you can reflect on your position with regard to the meaning of this industrial heritage vis-à-vis the new urban developments. You become involved, and the question arises of how you can influence those developments.

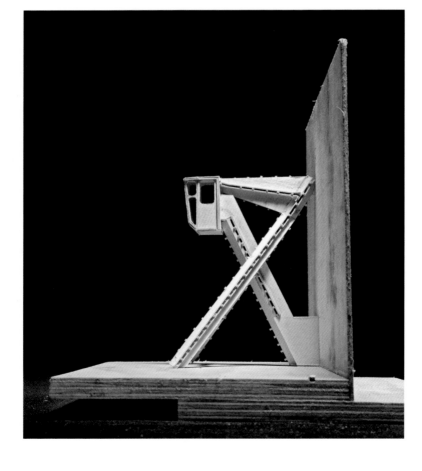

KAPKAR / SE-D2E

Project secretary's office
Date 2005
Location De Effenaar pop venue
Eindhoven, the Netherlands
Material new and recycled structural
plywood (Finnish pine), wooden
beams, lacquer

The office of pop venue De Effenaar with its beehive built-in furniture feels like the inside of one of those old bureaus full of drawers and compartments. The small room downstairs next to the main entrance was fitted out with a tailor-made system built of new and used plywood panels treated with different kinds of lacquer. The result is cosy and at the same time slightly claustrophobic. Wherever you look there are polygons. When you are working behind the desk it feels as though you are controlling the building like a pilot – which is actually the function of this secretariat: answering phone calls, receiving guests, selling tickets, operating the building lights, and viewing the security cameras.

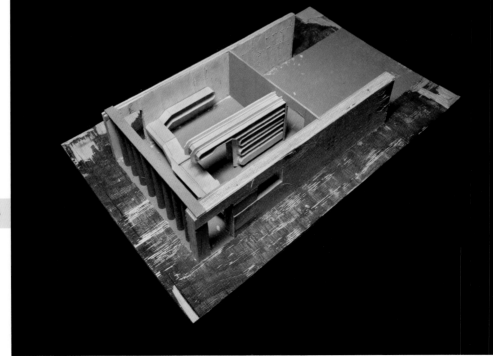

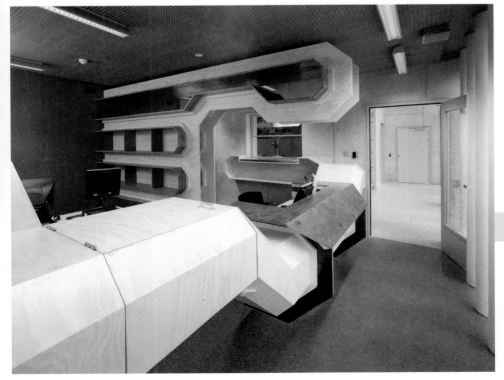

Project	treehouse
Date	2006
Client	Edith Ramakers and Lille Wagenmakers
Location	Westkapelle, the Netherlands
Material	structural plywood, polyester, Perspex / acrylic glass, metal beam

The treehouse is part of a farmhouse bed & breakfast and serves as a place to sleep. Havermans created the space specifically for this location and drew inspiration from the landscape of the province Zeeland. The form of the object is derived from the way in which dune vegetation grows in one particular direction because of the harsh onshore wind. The object balances on a round metal beam and the entrance is anchored to a concrete counterweight by connectors. The exterior of the treehouse is clad in polyester and its colour scheme alludes to the traditional farmhouses of Zeeland, which are black-tarred buildings with white frames. They have a practical purpose. In the dusk the black barns are invisible, but you can see the white window and door frames.

Project	cinema for two persons
Date	2007
Client	Netherlands Architecture Institute, Rotterdam, the Netherlands
Locations	7th São Paulo International Architecture Biennial; Design Week Vienna; Business of Design Week Hong Kong; Erasmushuis Jakarta, Indonesia; Museum of Modern Art, Arnhem, the Netherlands
Material	recycled construction multiplex, flat screen, film

KAPKAR / TT-C2P is a space developed for the 7th São Paulo International Architecture Biennial. Unlike art or design fairs, architecture exhibitions never show architecture. They mainly present representations of reality by means of photographs, scale models, renderings and films. *KAPKAR / TT-C2P* is not a representation of space, but an actual space that can be experienced as such. This two-person cinema has the appearance of a constructional sculptural space which continues in the interior. The seating and viewing angles in the interior are reflected in the construction and expose the function on the outside. The pattern of lines lies on the skin like a scarification. The 22-minute film that is screened inside is a montage of a series of thousands of photographs taken during a period of more than four weeks in Havermans' workshop, accompanied by a composition by Maarten van der Vleuten. To record the genesis of the cinema, a photograph was taken every 100 seconds around the clock during the production period. The film clearly shows that construction is an intense physical process in which a number of seemingly endless actions are repeated. The *KAPKAR / TT-C2P Cinema* is made to show itself. This idea touches on a theme in contemporary architecture that owes its raison d'être largely to its own professional field.

Project	multifunctional cabinet
Date	2008
Location	Advertising company X-Ingredient, 's-Hertogenbosch, the Netherlands
Material	construction plywood, white lacquer, orange Perspex 6 mm, screws / construction hangs on the brick wall and goes through into the hallway

This multifunctional cabinet is part of the new housing of advertising company X-Ingredient by Hilberink Bosch architecten. The assignment was to make an office cupboard for files, paper, boxes, and other typical office items. The almost industrial form of the cupboard swings through the space and fits itself around and through the existing holes in the brick partition between the hallway and the office space. One door entrance remained open, the other two former door entrances are closed with matted orange Perspex. The daylight from the office makes the diagonal part of the cabinet visible in the hallway shining through the Perspex sheets. In the office itself the orange Perspex changes intensity when the front door in the hallway is opened as clients enter or leave the building.

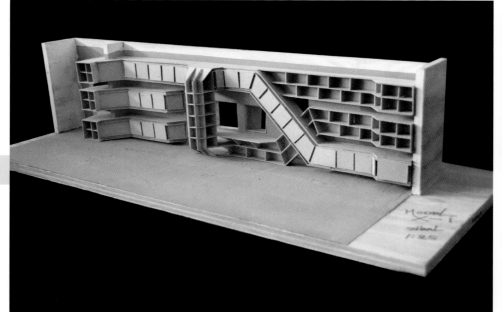

Hella Jongerius

Hella Jongerius

Finding a new balance between mass production in series and craft techniques has been a recurring theme in the work of Hella Jongerius (b. 1963) for many years. The production process is therefore an integral component of the concept. Her innovative combinations of materials and techniques are the key to pushing forward the boundaries of industrial production as well as traditional craftsmanship. Pivotal to this is finding a symbiosis between the flawlessness of mass production and the imperfection of manually crafted work. Jongerius sometimes deploys qualities that are traditionally associated with specific archetypes or materials in an alienating manner. This reinterpretation of existing forms underpins the design approach that Jongerius has adopted. The context is recurrently provided by the manufacturing history – in some cases extending back over centuries – of clients such as the Dutch ceramics firm Royal Tichelaar Makkum, the German porcelain manufacturer Nymphenburg and the New York-based textile supplier Maharam. Jongerius has drawn inspiration from their archives and existing models, decoration patterns, materials and techniques on several occasions, recasting them in a highly original concept. She also applies the principle of 'reinterpretation' to her own oeuvre, in which various products have evolved through a number of variants. Jongerius devotes most attention to earthenware, porcelain and textiles, and in recent years to furniture as well.

55

1.
Creating options

Text: Louise Schouwenberg
Graphic Design: Joost Grootens
Photography: Roel van Tour

The first thing that strikes a visitor to Nymphenburg, the German ceramics company, is the beauty and high quality of the traditional production process. While Jongerius did not always find the end products of the traditional manufacture attractive, and most of them seemed to be more suited to a different era, the production process itself was fascinating. The experiments with materials, glazes and shapes, the technical data which were generally stated on test pieces of materials and fired in the kiln with them, all these aspects which the general public never sees because they never leave the workshops, had an intrinsic beauty which she longed to translate into new products. She therefore not only collected existing patterns from the company's archives but also went in search of any visible tokens of the high quality of workmanship, fragments of drawings, colour tests and technical experiments. Then she had to talk the Nymphenburg craftsmen into transferring all those tokens of the company's expertise and potential, in fragments, to plates, bowls and dishes. The result displays a wide range of options, all those unsuspected possibilities which underlie any design process.

notes, written in 2003

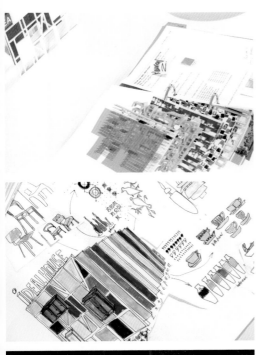

There is no such thing as an ideal house. After all, what can anybody want if the ideal solution has already been worked out? Ideal is by definition open, a projection into the future, and so it must remain. "I could say of my own house that at the present moment it works very well, and so is ideal for me. But can I really say that the same would be true for other people? And anyway, in my own house I keep all options open." Thus in 2005, when Jongerius was commissioned by the Cologne Furniture Fair to design 'the ideal house', she decided to look for a shape appropriate to the concept of 'changeability'. A changeability which embodied these histories and possibilities within itself. In the same way that every story is followed by a comma, so every table, chair and bench, every friend, training and job, every vase and every girlfriend is followed by a new desire.

In close cooperation with the architect Herman Verkerk and the designer Arian Brekveld (a senior Jongeriuslab designer) she filled an enormous filing cabinet with options. A visitor to Jongerius' 'ideal house' moved straight through suspended partitions hung behind one another like wings at the side of a stage. Each partition contained a file of memories and a storehouse of possibilities: chance finds from jumble sales, pieces of furniture which had been in the family for hundreds of years, disposable products and deliberately selected works by fellow designers. Besides a variety of products from her own files, Jongerius also showed her own work. What follows is a comma, ...

from the press release for 'Ideal House', Cologne 2005

The Backpack Sofa is a hybrid piece of furniture.
A marriage between a cupboard and a sofa,
a harmonious combination of down to earth
functionality and imaginative luxury. The sofa has
an elongated base bearing a pile of comfortable
pillows and blankets, slightly off centre, held together
with functional but decoratively appealing bands.

The extension to the back of the sofa refers, both
visually and functionally, to the backpacks worn by
diehard travellers. Like those bags, which are often
extremely well designed, this backpack mainly
contains options. How much weight can the
backpacker carry? How much surplus value can he
take with him on his journey? How much can be
stored in the Backpack Sofa? How high can one go?
It all depends, for instance on the needs and
imagination of the user.

press release for the Backpack Sofa, 2007

63

2.
Craft and industry

While the 21st century is characterised by globalisation, technological innovation and rapid networking, there is also a growing interest in traditions, age-old techniques and local crafts. It would be an oversimplification to associate these tendencies with a nostalgic yearning for the past.

In the Netherlands craftwork has experienced a new transformation, the nature of which has so far received little attention. We hardly have a classic traditional way of working, in which a process-oriented approach allows accidents to be utilised and controlled. Not surprisingly the visible traces of traditional manufacture in the work of conceptual designers refer not to the virtuoso genius of the maker's craftsmanship, but to the idea of genius and the idea of virtuoso craftsmanship. There is no greater gulf imaginable than that between the old masters and the present generation of Dutch designers. And this gulf will never be understood if the present attention paid to craftwork is interpreted purely as the continuation of a tradition.

from 'De stille kracht van de vormgeving' (The quiet strength of design) by Guus Beumer and Louise Schouwenberg in *Metropolis M*, nr.1, 2004

—

LOUISE You yourself have won fame with your emphasis on the making process and on the little flaws that occur.

HELLA I often use craft production methods. Even while I was a student, I experimented with so-called traditional materials like ceramics and textiles as well as with the high-tech stuff like polyurethane. I'm a firm believer in getting my hands dirty. I practically abuse the materials until I stumble into new ideas, new ways of seeing things. There is an incredible amount of intelligence involved in the making process itself. Trying to invent something by purely rational means rarely generates anything original, but working in my studio and pushing the envelope often yields surprises. So I let my materials and my intuition lead the way, and I put off looking for explanations to a later stage.

(…)

LOUISE And then you have to convince the industry people.

HELLA Yes, it's an approach that requires a lot of persuading. For example, I spent months at the EKWC (European Ceramic Work Centre) experimenting with firing temperatures, casting techniques, thicknesses, etcetera until I got exactly the kind of "flaws" I wanted for my *B-Set* china. Then I had to tackle the ceramics industry, and finally I succeeded in persuading Makkum to make the design. It was a real upheaval for them. I admire that company for applying their high standards of care and attention to making a product that clashes with their perfectionist culture.

(…)

HELLA Obviously, I count on a creative kind of consumer (ánd client), capable of connecting with my ideas, for example, with the story behind my *B-Set* china. There are plenty of people who prefer the old, cracked crocks from grandma's cupboard to a perfect new twelve-piece tea service. Even though my *B-Set* is produced serially, each individual piece is actually unique because they all have random flaws.

LOUISE And does that "story" amount to commitment? What I miss is the grand gesture. I hear much the same kind of story from amateur watercolorists and potters; they pour their heart and soul into their little masterpieces. You might as well do the same and just make one-offs in a small ceramic studio.

HELLA And sometimes I do, when a product calls for it. But I like the challenge of using industrial means to create an intelligent product with a high craft quality. I wish my work could make a major contribution to world events, but, really, I see the social role of the designer as being more modest. You talk of amateur potters and their woolly ambitions but then you're doing an injustice to the kind of involvement I'm looking for. Maybe the word commitment is a bit too strong, but designers are capable of arousing an interest in products and that's where my commitment lies.
I boost the individual character of the object, so to speak.

(…)

LOUISE …products that show traces of how they were made. But why does the visibility of the process and its fallibility result in a better product?

HELLA Because you elicit more involvement. The making process in itself isn't the most important thing. That may be the crucial mistake many ceramicists make in their work; they get a kick from kneading the clay but hardly concern themselves with whether what they are making is interesting. In my case, the making process is part of the concept, and you see that in the end result. It makes the user more aware of the relevance of the production process.

LOUISE So that's why you prefer craft techniques?

HELLA It's an obvious choice, of course. But it's an approach you can apply to industrial products and new, high-tech materials as well. People are fed up with all the throwaway rubbish and long for things that have some significance to them.

from 'A conversation that might have taken place', *Hella Jongerius*, Phaidon, 2003

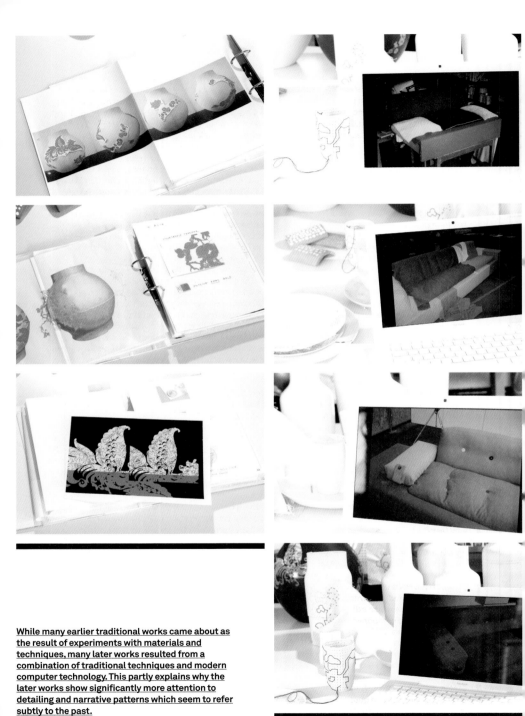

While many earlier traditional works came about as the result of experiments with materials and techniques, many later works resulted from a combination of traditional techniques and modern computer technology. This partly explains why the later works show significantly more attention to detailing and narrative patterns which seem to refer subtly to the past.

notes for a text on Craft, *Metropolis M*, nr.6, 2004

—

The leitmotif running through Jongerius' work is the search for a good compromise between plain, mass-produced items and handmade and often richly decorated one-offs. Perhaps nothing has tested this ambition better than the four large vases she designed for Ikea.

My products are often seen as a comment on the industrial approach. And yes, I do resist the neutral perfection and conformity we often associate with industrial production. But instead of rejecting that approach I want to look for solutions within industry. If I can spare the time and attention required for the best traditional techniques I can safely rely on the individual character of the items I produce. But if I can get a similar result by industrial methods it will mean much more. The apparent antagonism offers great charm. I therefore search for the right compromise which will allow me to combine the advantages of a unique handmade piece with those of a serially produced product. I would never deny the connection between design and serial reproduction.

Your products can be found in museums and private collections all over the world. Apart from institutional buyers only well-to-do design lovers can afford them: the prices are simply too high for the average citizen. Your products could be compared with works of art, which are also aimed primarily at an exclusive market and specific target groups. Until recently you seemed to have had no ambition to serve a larger market, like the one served by Ikea. Does working for Ikea signify a break in your professional practice? A move from design which is essentially artistic to design for the masses?

I don't consider it a break. I do both: I work on commissions for companies and create one-offs when required by the design process. If I had worked for Ikea at the beginning of my career the results would definitely not have been great. I was quite happy to design ceramic vases for them because I feel that I have developed everything there is to be developed in that field. I was able to use the knowledge and experience I had gathered over the years to design low-cost vases which still bear my personal stamp. Working for a company like Ikea definitely means having to work within the limits they specify, especially on price. In this respect companies like Maharam and Vitra are quite different. The market they aim at is more exclusive. In a way that makes things easier for me. But basically the task remains the same: finding a way to do justice to the requirement for a quality which meets my standards within an industrial process.

What was the production process like at Vitra?

After an exploring conversation I got the commission to design a sofa. A sofa! The most dreadful product! Just like many people I sought for years to find one for my home. Most of them are downright ugly. A large block-system foam. After my first fright I decided to accept the challenge and design a sofa which I myself would gladly place in my house. I started with some requirements in my head: no block-system foam, it had to be comfortable, variable and also the tactile quality was of paramount importance. Arian Brekveld (designer in Jongeriuslab) and I embedded gentle cushions of several fabrics, colors, altitudes, in a harder podium around them. Because of the landscape appearance I called the sofa Polder, referring to the tracts of land reclaimed from the sea in Holland.

Concessions?

I wouldn't call them concessions. There was never a conflict between us and Vitra. … As it turned out, we all wanted the same thing. Vitra is a fantastic company to work with. What mattered was achieving the best possible result. The experience was similar to the experience I had with Maharam, for which I designed fabrics in the Repeat range. If a company has vision and is enthusiastic about working with me, the end result will satisfy everyone involved.

Apart from differences in the nature of the product and price, is there anything different about working for Ikea?

Essentially the process is the same. As at Vitra, the Ikea people were totally committed to achieving the best possible result. Maybe it took slightly more effort on my part to get the exact quality I wanted while knowing that the vases would be mass-produced. Some parts were handmade, which takes time. They were made in China, because costs are low there. When the first products were shipped to Europe, some small components turned out to be not quite right. I could simply have accepted them, because they really were not as bad as all that, but instead we decided to go to China to ensure that all the necessary improvements were made.

It's a well-known marketing strategy to have famous designers working for large companies.

True, many companies engage designers as a crazy artistic gesture over and above their usual business, simply to improve their image. I wouldn't settle for that. Both Vitra and Ikea made a conscious choice to work with me. They gave me all the freedom I needed to produce a serious product, not a one time gadget. Currently I'm working on the completion of my furniture collection for Vitra.

from 'Q + A Hella Jongerius', in *I.D. magazine*, 2006

3.
Treasures from the archives

As a designer, Hella Jongerius firmly believes that justice is best done to treasures from the past by setting them in a modern context. She takes the best from two worlds and combines them to create a marvellous symbiosis. Sometimes she chooses patterns and materials which she finds in the records of companies such as the Dutch ceramics factory Tichelaar, the German ceramics company Nymphenburg or the American fabric manufacturer Maharam, or a museum such as the Cooper Hewitt museum in New York. Then she might mix them with contemporary personal details, such as the technical details of the traditional and industrial process and her own personal stamp. Options from the past, including decorative patterns, generate new meanings by being approached from today's perspective.

In 2005, at the request of Tichelaar in Makkum, Friesland, Jongerius reacted to one of the firm's existing products, the Majolica dishes which were produced in great numbers between 1700 and 1890 and even today form part of the firm's assortment. These were cheap, coarsely decorated products, intended for everyday use. The undersides of the dishes were generally covered with a cheap transparent lead glaze, while the tops were tin-glazed and bore a simple painting. The glaze was applied by dipping the pieces into it. Jongerius decided to give a fresh lease of life to both the pattern and the technique. She arranged to have parts of her dishes dipped into the glaze (and applied the majolica patterns to those parts) and left the remainder bare. The result displayed both the typical Majolica decoration and clay, the firm's most basic raw material.

notes, written in 2007

HELLA …You consciously avoid designing new forms but you add a new dimension, a different function or a different story. That's like what I do. When I get a commission from Maharam, I don't rush to my drawing board to design a snazzy new pattern. I pore through the archives, use existing patterns, and add a new concept to them.

(…)

HELLA I must admit I am a blatant aesthete. The concept is uppermost in the end, but on the way I am largely occupied with the general appearance. I fiddle about endlessly with colors and dimensions, agonize about which layer to put over the other, and which pattern against which color.

LOUISE Aren't you undermining your own 'story' with those aesthetics?

HELLA I realize it's a danger, but I think I deal with it by getting <u>my aesthetics from things that have long ago proved their worth, from things with a history.</u> The Museum Boijmans Van Beuningen commissioned me to design new products using antique pot shards from their collection. The bright red car paint I sprayed right over the shards and the new vase form was devilishly beautiful, of course. What is more, it created a marvelous combination of old and new.

from 'A conversation that might have taken place', *Hella Jongerius*, Phaidon, 2003

73

—
Today, in 2007, stories, meanings, experiments with materials and compromises between one-off and mass-produced products still characterise Jongerius' work. But something has changed. For a recent project (Layers) for Maharam and for Ikea (still to be realised) she created the decorative patterns herself rather than selecting them from existing archival material or from the iconography of earlier Jongerius products. Yet the central issue remains the relationship between old and new, past and present. The patterns devised by Jongerius refer to pieces of history, real or imaginary, or to records which might or might not exist.

notes, written in 2007

4.
Pushing the limits of the design field

—

Design is a matter of image, of meanings that transcend purpose and utility, and of context.

Design has always been concerned with functionality and industrial reproduction, not with one-offs or small series with artistic pretensions. These kinds of things are the business of the traditional disciplines and the visual arts.

In the last century the concept of functionality evolved from an instrumental concept into a concept that leaves scope for added value. Design is concerned with image, meaning and narrative force, qualities which since time immemorial have been associated with the visual arts.

The only thing required of design is the production of added value. In this sense design - partly because of its serial character - has become an extremely satisfactory response to art. In the last ten years this added value has been the result of an increased awareness of its own functioning.

Added value, rather than functionality, is the first and perhaps even the only goal of design. Instead of a possible retreat into a private design world and the forecast return to functionalism, design seems more likely to appropriate other fields of activity to ensure the permanent provision of added cultural value and so of economic worth.

Throughout the 20th century, functionality gave the design profession its self-evident right to exist, a quality that in the 1980s was much less applicable to the visual arts. While art began to experience a crisis of legitimacy, products, besides functionality, turned out to represent more artistic worth than had previously been suspected, with the result that designers became more ambitious. The professional practices of top designers began to look like those previously associated with artists. Design products

became increasingly valued as expressions in their own right, and were displayed in the media and in contexts which had previously been reserved exclusively for the arts. Slowly but surely instrumental functionality was to fade away as the most important condition for design. Moreover the display of design in museums and the visual media demanded a different kind of visual quality than that provided by functionality and comfort. In consequence the importance of a powerful iconography was to increase sharply, which led to the unfamiliar situation for the profession that some products appeared more often in magazines than in users' homes.

The fact that many products never got further than the prototype stage seemed to disturb neither designers nor lovers of design. The ordinary user has even ceased to be the most attractive consumer of contemporary design. This position has been taken over by art collectors, museums and design devotees who can afford to pay astronomic prices for one-offs or small series.

Paradoxically, the functionality of Office Pets lies in their lack of utility. These strange objects, shown for the first time by Vitra at the Limited Editions exhibition during the Miami Basel Art Fair in 2007, refer both to the imagination and to the tightly and efficiently ordered world of corporate identities.

The surfaces of these wooden tables, dating from 2007, shown in the Kreo gallery in Paris, blended with shapes that were half abstract, half animal. These sculptural tables seem to challenge the difference between art and design. They are equally at home in both worlds, yet Jongerius says quite explicitly that they are functional objects, not works of art.

from 'Limited Substance', a text on Limited Editions for *Frame Magazine*, September 2007

—

HELLA At least your colleagues give you flowers when you have something to celebrate. That never happens if you're a designer. <u>Who'd want to ruin a perfectly good vase by putting flowers in it?</u>

LOUISE Yes, artists get flowers, and then they just grab the nearest pot or bucket to put them in. But it's noticeable that the people who design vases never get flowers. So why do designers design vases?

HELLA Because of the "stories" they tell. Vases were originally meant to be used, of course, but like any useful object <u>a vase has a potential that goes beyond functionality. The story can rise above the object itself.</u>

LOUISE Then you're talking about art.

HELLA No, I'm not talking about art. Useful objects have a rich history. They are saturated with references to specific contexts and specific moments in history. If you refer to that history explicitly and include all the associations in a new story, then you are communicating something, and it's something about useful objects.

LOUISE But if it isn't the use that's really important, only your ideas about the significance of the object, why don't you, say, drill a hole in the bottom of the vase? If you work with the pretensions of an artist, why don't you simply ignore functionality?

HELLA I don't believe I have artistic pretensions. Design is my thing. Most of my designs are actually usable, and only occasionally do I completely ignore the actual use. When I decorate cups with embroidery that goes right through the porcelain,

I obviously realize you can't drink tea out of them. But that isn't really so important because you could think up a different function for the cups.

LOUISE So the ideas more or less force you to reduce the functionality?

HELLA Embroidery gives me a way of saying something about customs of eating and decorating, about being trapped in conventions and etiquette.

LOUISE Does the balance sometimes tip the other way? Can the function be uppermost?

HELLA I'm happiest when the design works well in all respects. If, on top of that, it's also suitable for mass production, it's a real kick. <u>I like the industrial process</u>; art can't compete with the scale industry works on. The commission I had from the textile company Maharam brought all these issues together nicely. Besides the design work and the large-scale execution, it also involved me in the adventure of marketing.
(…)
I test the boundaries of ideas that are current at the moment.
(…)
LOUISE You mean chic designers who make stupid vases that would be better hidden under massive bunches of flowers? Do only vases with a strong intellectual content belong on pedestals, then?

HELLA I'm not in favor of pedestals, literally, of course. But good design can measure up against fine art—it must.

from 'A conversation that might have taken place', *Hella Jongerius*, Phaidon, 2003

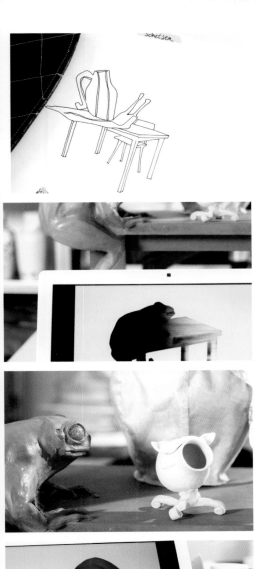

—
How much autonomy can a functional object stand?
Only when contemporary everyday objects dare
to cross the boundary between utility and relative
artistic autonomy do they have the potential to both
deny themselves, in the Heideggerian sense
(disappearing in their reliability), and prove
themselves at the same time. They fulfil their promise
as functional objects while vigorously asserting
themselves as vehicles of meaning.

part of a lecture for the symposium 'The Politics of
Design' which took place in Centraal Museum Utrecht,
September 2007

"My vases are not just for holding a flower. I hope that it also conveys an *experience*. I want people to build up relations with objects, to mingle with them. Because it is only then that you keep them with you and want to cherish them.

It is a theme that has occupied me for a long time. I am convinced that it is difficult for something completely new to stick. 'Gimmicky', you probably think and then walk on. A combination of the new with the old works better. The love of old things belongs to every age, just like recollections. They offer security, make a connection between you and the outside world. They provide an emotion, a feeling of recognition and security that makes you open up to the unknown. That is why I like to use archives and, as a part of them, archetypal forms.

Another way to achieve the communication that I aim for is the human dimension of things. That scale is timeless too. People do not want to feel excluded. You can incorporate the human scale by working in a craftsmanlike way – in other words, with attention and an eye for detail. Details – in the *Polder Sofa* they are large knots of natural material – betray the personal signature of the designer. This individual character has become a quality standard that is here to stay, I am absolutely convinced of that. Innovative companies fell for it years ago and 'the' market consists by now of niches.

However, for me quality goes beyond working in a craftsmanlike way alone. Quality is a wide-ranging term. It arises when a product has been thought out at every level: in its function, its aesthetics, its kind of material, its method of production, its price. All of these aspects are causally linked with one another. Especially in my work for industrial clients, such as Vitra or IKEA, the fine tuning calls for inventiveness. It is a fascinating quest. The narrower the road becomes, the more creative you have to be. That is when the radars really start to work."

Products
2002-2009

Soft Urn

Product	vase
Material	polyurethane
Colours	natural, pink
Produced and	
distributed by	Jongeriuslab

Jongerius' fascination with the effect and perception of synthetic materials prompted her to research how rubber might assimilate an opposite quality such as old age. Moulding the rubber in an archetypical form and then giving it the colour of medieval glass resulted in an unrecognizable modern-day variant of the vase. This realization only begins to grow on actually touching the vase, when its form proves to be elastic. Jongerius designed a younger version of the *Soft Urn* in 1999, simply by making it pink.

Product	pot
Material	porcelain, epoxy, stoneware
Colours	white, silver, red, terra
Produced by	Jongeriuslab
	unique pieces

Using medieval shards donated by the Museum Boijmans Van Beuningen, Jongerius took the initiative in a restoration project. She created seven archetypes in which she glued the shards with epoxy. Some parts of the vases and pots were painted in bright colours; old and new were joined together. The pots were decorated with porcelain labels of Jongerius' thumbprint and other ceramic data. This was customary in the Middle Ages when illiterate potters would mark their pots with their fingerprints on the underside.

B-set Dinner Service

Product	service
Material	porcelain
Colour	white
Produced and	
distributed by	Royal Tichelaar Makkum, the Netherlands

Jongerius has deliberately introduced irregularities in her porcelain dinner service, deformed by extremely high temperatures in the kiln. As a result every single piece of the *B-set Dinner Service* has acquired a unique identity because of its irregular shape. The recipe for the porcelain and the glaze are stamped in the forms to illustrate the recipe culture in the world of ceramics. It is a seven-piece service and consists of a bowl, a saucer, a large and a small cup, a large and a small plate, and a water jug.

Big White Pot and Red / White Vase

Product	pot, vase
Material	porcelain
Colours	white, red
Produced and	
distributed by	Royal Tichelaar Makkum,
	the Netherlands

In 1998 two pots from the series *7 pots / 3 centuries / 2 materials* were cast in porcelain. In both cases the casting seams were still clearly visible as if the pots consisted of several pieces.

Long Neck and Groove Bottles

Product	bottle
Material	glass, porcelain, packing tape
Colours	blank, coloured
Produced and distributed by	Jongeriuslab

Examining the idea of families of objects in which each individual item has its own, distinct personality, Jongerius began thinking about the similarities between glass and ceramics. Both materials are based on earth – sand or clay – and both need heat in order to be transformed.

Jongerius experimented with ways to combine the two materials. The porcelain vase was created at first and then used to make a mould for the glass vase. The result is two separate vases with two separate identities, though each is made to fit with the other. To connect the two elements, they were wrapped together with bright packing tape, which is usually used for packaging fragile objects. As a result the modern plastic tape has become the most constructive part of a vase that consists of two precious age-old materials.

Embroidered Tablecloth

Product tablecloth
Material linen, cotton, porcelain plate
Colours white, grey, red
Produced by Jongeriuslab
limited edition

The *Embroidered Tablecloth* is part of a series of products inspired by two ceramic works from the collection of the Museum Princessehof in Leeuwarden: a 14th-century copper vase from China and a 15th-century cobalt blue Ming vase. Jongerius does not simply adopt their form but also draws inspiration from their decoration. She punches in decorative forms like dragons and floral motifs, embroiders them or fills them with rubber to make them watertight. Jongerius sees a close tie between ceramics decorations and textile techniques such as embroidery. In the *Embroidered Tablecloth* Jongerius liberates both techniques from their original context and materials by simply allowing them to blend with one another.

Repeat Classic and Repeat Dot

Product   upholstery fabric
Material   viscose, cotton
Produced and
distributed by   Maharam, USA

The upholstery fabric *Repeat* incorporates different patterns. Jongerius did not design these patterns herself, but used a collection of classic motifs instead. These are not repeated every 30 centimetres, the norm in the textile industry, but every 300 centimetres. In addition, technical data is printed on the fabric, with the dotted patterns as references to the perforated cards that are traditionally used to programme the weaving looms. Though the fabric is produced industrially, this feature alludes to the craft aspect of the production process. The material was commissioned by the New York-based textile manufacturer Maharam, which asked Jongerius to design a fabric so that every piece of furniture upholstered would be unique while still forming an ensemble.

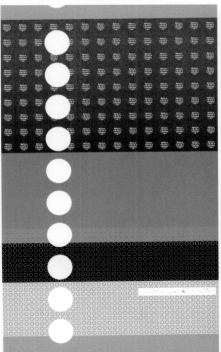

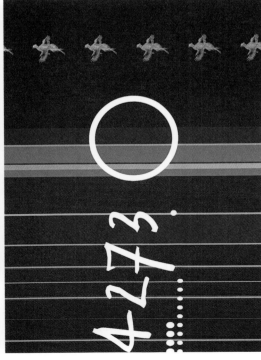

Product bowl, plate
Material porcelain
Produced and
distributed by Nymphenburg Porcelain
Manufactory, Germany

The Nymphenburg Porcelain Manufactory has been in continuous operation since 1761 and has built up a collection of more than 30,000 designs, from which Jongerius chose historical decors and animal figures as the theme for her plate and bowl designs. Both the plates and the bowls are created exclusively by hand and no two plates are identical. They vary in size and depth and the marks left behind by the craftwork remain visible.

Polder Sofa

Product sofa

Material wooden frame with belt upholstery, backrest cushions: polyurethane chips and microfibres, textured surface and seat cushion: polyurethane foam and polyester/wool, armrest with sand weights, buttons made of natural materials

Colours red, green, anthracite, dark brown, crème

Produced and distributed by Vitra, Basel

The design and name of the sofa is a reference to the flat polder landscape of the Netherlands. The elongated carcass of this asymmetrically arranged sofa is similarly low and flat, and emphasizes the horizontal. The cushions and carcass are upholstered in five different fabrics in five coordinating colours. Large buttons decorating the cushions are unmistakable trademarks of the *Polder Sofa* and are made of natural materials like bone and mother of pearl. The buttons are sewn to the cushions with bold, broad cross stitches.

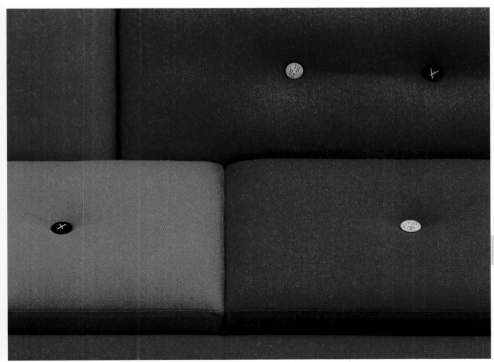

93

Product	bowl, plate, vase, candleholder
Material	porcelain decorated with majolica technique
Produced and distributed by	Royal Tichelaar Makkum, the Netherlands

The *Non-Temporary* earthenware bowls, plates, vases and candleholders are made from the Frisian marine clay found near Royal Tichelaar's factories and are decorated with glazing and painting techniques that the company has used since the 17th century.

Jonsberg

Product vase

Material porcelain, earthenware, terracotta, stoneware

Produced and distributed by Ikea, Sweden

This assignment put Jongerius' pursuit of uniqueness within Ikea's large-scale production to the test in a positive manner. Every vase has been produced by hand. This was possible because Ikea has manufacturing operations in China that produce very high-quality handwork but can also deal with large volumes.

The four vases all have an identical shape, a familiar archetypal vase form. Every vase has a pattern that represents a particular part of the world, and each pattern is applied using a specific ceramic technique.

Product	wall hanging
Material	wool, cotton, polyester
Produced and	
distributed by	Ikea, Sweden

Jongerius created wall hangings for Ikea, which are embroidered with the imaginative images of a goat, a fox and a rabbit, and refer to the local roots of Ikea as the depicted animals feature in Swedish fairy tales. In the production process large scale industrial production by Ikea is combined with small scale craft production in India. The wall hangings are part of the Ikea-Unicef programme, which helps women in India to start up small sewing businesses and enables their children to go to school. The result consists of textiles of which not only Ikea and Jongerius will benefit, but also the craftswomen who left their traces in the making. On the back of the work is a label with the names of Ikea, Hella Jongerius and the embroidered name of the woman who contributed to the handcrafted parts.

IKEA Mikkel

Product wall hanging
Material wool, cotton, polyester
Produced and
distributed by Ikea, Sweden

Product	wall hanging
Material	wool, cotton, polyester
Produced and distributed by	Ikea, Sweden

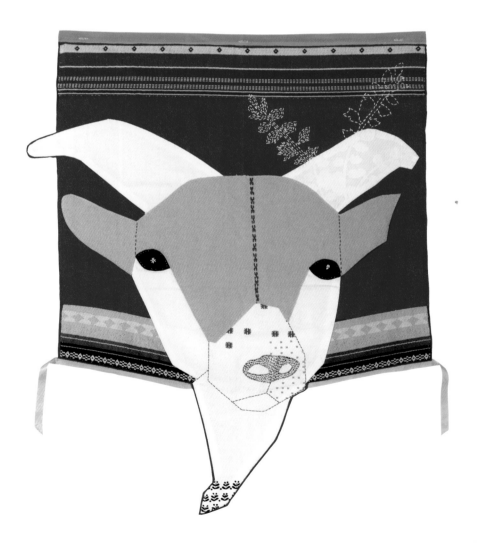

Natura Design Magistra

Product   table
Material   wood (walnut), grey epoxy finish
Produced by   Jongeriuslab
                   limited edition

Jongerius has become known for the way she explores the possibilities and boundaries of both handicraft and industrial techniques and subsequently stretches them beyond the already known. By exploiting coincidence and even mistakes in the production process she succeeds to accomplish uniqueness within the industrial production. Apart from this fascination for techniques and materials, the narrative quality of products plays a mayor role in her work. Stories seem to hide underneath the skin of products, due to the reinterpretation of historical decorative patterns, but also due to the imaginative use of the images of flowers and animals. Decoration mediates between man and object to tighten the bond. In the Frog table the decoration has expanded beyond the surface, stressing both the sculptural and the imaginative quality of this piece of furniture.

Claudy Jongstra

Claudy Jongstra

Claudy Jongstra (b. 1963) first fell under the spell of felt in 1994. Her many years of experimentation with felting techniques has been motivated by a limitless fascination for the traditional production process, the durable and technical possibilities of wool. The result is an extraordinary palette of textiles that are as rugged as they are refined, in which felt is completely stripped of its traditionally frumpy image. Jongstra's urge to experiment has greatly expanded the arsenal of possibilities with felt: she combines wool from various animal species and different breeds of sheep, but also creates felt that mixes wool with materials such as silk and even metal. Jongstra keeps the entire process from raw materials to end product in her own hands, so that she can operate independently and, more especially, to be able to work sustainable. Jongstra tends her own flock of rare Drenthe Heath sheep, thus contributing to the survival of this age-old breed in the Netherlands. Establishing her own dyeworks has made it possible for her to colour her products with natural dyestuffs rather than synthetic ones. The overall controllability of the process stands in stark contrast to the element of chance that is inherent of the process of making felt. Jongstra's textiles are used by various fashion designers, but at the moment her most important projects involve the embellishment of the interiors of buildings with rugs and wall coverings.

Wool

Durability - Wool is durable. The fibre is exceptionally strong and woollen objects can last for years.

Insulation - Wool insulates. The special structure of the fibre ensures that heat is retained. Besides insulating against cold, wool also provides sound insulation.

Beautiful - Wool is beautiful. The beauty of wool is a combination of the exceptional fibre, the rich variegation, the durability, the warmth and the flexibility.

Natural - Wool is a natural product. This means that wool is hypoallergenic and can be used in environments where stringent hygiene standards have to be met.

Strong - Wool is strong. Wool fibre can be bent and twisted infinitely without breaking it. A high elasticity makes wool even stronger.

Elastic - Wool is elastic and springy. The special structure of the fibre and the high capacity to retain its original form mean that wool feels soft, gives easily and is a pleasure to process.

Versatile - Wool is versatile. It has numerous uses thanks to its wonderful properties. Wool can be employed for its beauty, warmth, safety, acoustic properties and much more besides. In addition to its use for apparel, wool is also used for buildings, for coverings and insulation, for works of art and industrial applications.

Breathable - Wool breathes. The fibre has a water-repellent surface and a core with an exceptionally high absorptivity.

Fire-resistant - Wool is resistant to fire. The fibre has a high ignition temperature and an exceptionally slow combustion rate.

Self-cleaning - Wool cleans itself. The exceptional structure of the fibre and its high fat content means that wool picks up dirt less quickly and contaminants are expelled by the fibre itself when it is exposed to moist air.

Felt

Felt is a non-woven textile, produced by compacting fibres into a matted fabric. There are three ingredients needed to make felt: wool, water and soap. The first stage in the felting process is to lay out several layers of tufts of wool. Rubbing water and soap into the wool makes the fibres interlock, and the friction of continued rubbing results in the formation of felt. Felt is in all probability the first textile fabricated by mankind. The oldest surviving felt artefacts, and those considered most important by experts, originated from Persia in the period 600-200 BC and were found in Pazyryk tombs in Siberia.

Species / Breeds / Materials

Claudy Jongstra's urge to experiment has greatly
expanded the arsenal of possibilities with felt: she
combines wool from various animal species and different
breeds of sheep, but also creates felt that mixes wool with
materials such as silk and even metal.

Alpaca

Species	Huacaya and Suri (*Vicugna Pacos*)
Family	Camelidae
Genus	Vicugna
Main location	Andes Mountains, Southern Peru
Main use	wool
Withers height	90 cm (adult males)
Weight	61 kg (adult males)

The Alpaca lives on the upland plains of Bolivia and particularly Peru. The animal has a withers height of 90 centimetres with a long coat that often extends down to the ground. The fleece occurs in more than 22 distinct colour shades. The Alpaca is principally raised for the wool. There are two subspecies that differ only in the type of wool: the Huacaya has a soft, slightly curly fleece and the Suri has long, thick strands.

Cashmere

Breed name	Changthangi (also Kashmiri or Pashmina Goat)
Main group	Mountain Goat
Subgroup	Himalayan Mountain Goat
Main location	Ladakh, Kashmir, India (specifically Changthangi)
Main use	1. meat
	2. wool
	3. transport
Withers height	49 cm (adult males), 52 cm (adult females)
Weight	20 kg (adult males), 19 kg (adult females)

Cashmere is a generic name for all wool that is thinner than 19 microns in diameter. Most Cashmere wool is between 16 and 18 microns. Pashmina wool has the thinnest, finest fibres, with a diameter of between 12 and 14 microns. Cashmere wool comes from the Himalayan Mountain Goat. A goat produces no more than 90 grams of wool per year. In the spring these goats shed their winter coat for a summer coat. The wool is collected by plucking it from the rocks and shrubs or by brushing the goats.

Cotton Gauze

Lengths of cotton gauze are used as an underlay for making the felt or to give the felt a specific appearance.

Drenthe Heath Sheep

Dutch name	Drents Heideschaap
Main group	Heath Group
Subgroup	Dutch Heath
Main location	Province of Drenthe, the Netherlands
Main use	1. vegetation management
	2. meat
	3. wool
Withers height	52 cm (adult males), 47 cm (adult females)
Weight	50 kg (adult males), 45 kg (adult females)

The Drenthe Heath sheep is the oldest breed in continental Western Europe. The breed has been reared in the Netherlands, primarily in the Province of Drenthe, since 4000 BC, when it was introduced by migrants, probably from France. The Drenthe Heath breed is a sheep that is still close to nature, requiring little care and displays a high degree of independence. With a withers height of approximately 52 centimetres this breed is the smallest sheep in the Netherlands. The Drenthe Heath breed is subdivided into old and new subtypes. The rare old type has a slim build, so it can manoeuvre easily across less easily accessible natural terrains. Its legs are slim and tough, with sinewy joints. The head has a

short, straight nasal profile and matt, stiff hair, while the crown is covered with stiff, curly hair. The tail extends far below the hocks and has a thick covering of wool. The new Drenthe type is most common and resulted from crossbreeding the old type with amongst others the Schoonebeek breed. The new type therefore has a 'ram nose' and has lustrous hair on its head and legs. The wool is long and tough, but an experienced spinner can transform it into wonderful yarns. It is the only Dutch sheep breed with horned rams, and it displays a great assortment of colours: fox reds, browns, blacks, black- and brown-speckled heads, as well as mottled combinations. The lambs are often born with mottled coats, but the colour of the fleece becomes increasingly grey as they mature into adults.

The Drenthe Heath sheep was primarily raised for its manure, which was indispensable for arable farming. Many flocks of sheep became redundant with the introduction of chemical fertilizers. Nowadays the Drenthe Heath breed is only raised for historical reasons and for grazing heathland areas and dunes as a maintenance measure.

Merino Sheep

Breed name	Spanish Merino
Main group	Merino
Subgroup	Iberian Merino
Main location	Andalusia, Spain and Estremadura, Portugal
Main use	1. meat
	2. wool
	3. fur
Withers height	82 cm (adult males), 77 cm (adult females)
Weight	83 kg (adult males), 52 kg (adult females)

The Merino sheep is one of the most renowned and most widespread breeds of sheep in the world. It is, however, a rarity in the Netherlands. The Merino breed originates from sheep kept by a small Berber tribe in North Africa that was conquered by the Spanish. The Spanish took the sheep breed with them and crossbred it with Spanish

sheep, which eventually resulted in the breed we know today. Merino sheep are primarily renowned for their wool. Thanks to its many folds of skin, a single sheep produces no less than five kilograms of wool per year. The Merino sheep is not only outstanding in its high wool production, but also in the wool's exceptional quality. A Merino sheep has ten times as many little hairs per square centimetre of skin as the average for other sheep. The wool has a very fine structure and is therefore highly suitable for numerous uses.

Raw Linen

Rough, unprocessed linen consisting of strands approximately 18 centimetres in length.

Raw Silk

Raw, unprocessed silk consisting of strands that are about 20 centimetres long.

Schoonebeek Sheep

Dutch name	Schoonebeeker
Main group	Heath Group
Subgroup	Dutch Heath
Main location	Southeast part of the Province of Drenthe, the Netherlands
Main use	1. vegetation management
	2. meat
	3. wool
Withers height	77 cm (adult males), 72 cm (adult females)
Weight	80 kg (adult males), 50 kg (adult females)

The Schoonebeek breed is named after the Dutch town of Schoonebeek in the southeast of the Province of Drenthe. It is highly likely that the Schoonebeek breed is descended from Bentheimer sheep, which were raised just across the border in Germany. The Schoonebeek is not the oldest heath sheep breed, but at the moment it is the rarest breed of Dutch origin. The Schoonebeek makes very few demands with regard to diet, care and shelter. The many years of natural selection in the midst of rugged terrain has made the breed strong, resilient and sober. The Schoonebeek sheep is the largest of the Dutch heath breeds. The sheep has a distinctly elegant appearance because of the long neck and the high, uplifted head. Its relatively long and slender head has a highly typical 'ram nose', a rounded nasal bone that is also known as a Roman nose. The ears are large and set high on the head. The breed is long-legged and the legs are thin, but are tough and dry like those of a deer.

111

The coat of hair on head and legs is short, shiny and devoid of wool. The tail is woollen and reaches to below the hocks. The fleece is long and straight, with a hairy structure.

The lambs are almost always born with well-defined light-dark contrasts. All manner of colour variations are to be found, such as a brown-black mottling, dark reddish brown, white, black with a blaze, and black. The colour of the fleece is almost always an off-white or in a few cases black. The mottled colours remain visible on the head and legs. A rarely seen colour variant is a light reddish brown. Schoonebeek sheep in this warm orange hue often remain slightly smaller and slimmer than their contemporaries and are known as 'Ommertjes'.

Silk Chiffon

Silk chiffon is a thin, transparent, flowing plain-woven textile.

Silk Metallic Organza

Silk organza with metallic thread to strengthen the weave. Oxidization of the metal means that the colour of the fabric alters over the years.

Silk Organza

Silk organza is a thin, transparent, stiff plain-weave textile.

Wensleydale

Breed name	Wensleydale
Main group	British Longwool Group
Main location	Great Britain
Main use	1. meat
	2. wool
Withers height	89 cm (adult males), 82 cm (adult females)
Weight	126 kg (adult males), 90 kg (adult females)

The Wensleydale Longwool is a fairly rare breed that was originally raised in North Yorkshire, England. At the moment the breed is primarily found in the Yorkshire Dales, North Lancashire, Westmorland, Cumberland and parts of Scotland. The breed has never become very widespread and for a long time it was even listed as endangered. The Wensleydale is a hardy breed. The breed's most remarkable feature is its long, curly wool. The wool is transparent, lustrous and strong. The sheep is completely covered in fleece with the exception of part of the head (though it does have wool on the crown and the cheeks) and the ears. Head, ears, nose and legs are dark blue in colour. The ears are large and set fairly high on the head, while the neck is long. Wensleydale sheep are a long-legged breed.

Yak

Species	Yak (Bos grunniens)
Family	Bovidae
Genus	Bos
Main location	Himalaya Mountains, Tibet
Main use	1. transport
	2. wool
Withers height	167 cm (adult males), 137 cm (adult females)
Weight	612 kg (adult males), 294 kg (adult females)

The yak is a long-haired bovine found throughout the Himalayan region of south Central Asia. They have long shaggy hair to insulate them from the cold. Yak fibres are soft and smooth and occur in several colours, including shades of grey, brown, black and white. It is combed or shed from the yak and then de-haired, resulting in a splendid downy fibre that can be spun into yarn for knitting.

Natural Dyestuffs

Jongstra only uses natural dyestuffs to colour her textiles. Since the Second World War natural dyestuffs have been completely superseded by synthetic ones.

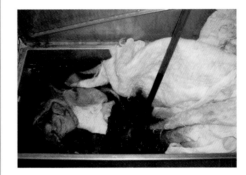

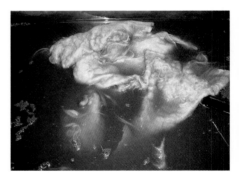

Reds

English name	Common Madder
Dutch name	Meekrap
Family	Rubiaceae
Genus	Rubia
Species	Tinctorum
Origin	Europe

There are about 35 species of madder, ranging in height from 1 to 3 metres. In Europe the plants are left in the soil for 24 to 30 months. The madder roots are long and about as thick as a lead pencil. Madder was once the main cotton dye in Europe and was extensively cultivated in Europe, including France and the Netherlands, and in the Middle East for a range of red to purple dyes obtained from the rhizome.

Colour Swatches

The effect of Madder on different kinds of wool

Yellows

English name	Weld (Dyer's Rocket)
Dutch name	Wouw
Family	Resedaceae
Genus	Reseda
Species	Luteola
Origin	Mediterranean region

Weld, or Dyer's rocket, is a biennial herb and the plant is longest known as a source of yellow dye in the world. It grows to a height of between 30 and 100 centimetres and is common on wasteland and in ploughed fields on chalky soil. It has an unbranched or slightly branched stem with long, spathulate leaves. The flowers are pale yellow and usually consist of four sepals and four petals. The flowering period is June to September. Weld is indigenous to the Mediterranean region but is now also found in many other parts of the world. The plant used to be widely cultivated for its dye. Every part of the plant can be used for dyestuffs except for the roots.

Colour Swatches

The effect of Weld on different kinds of wool.

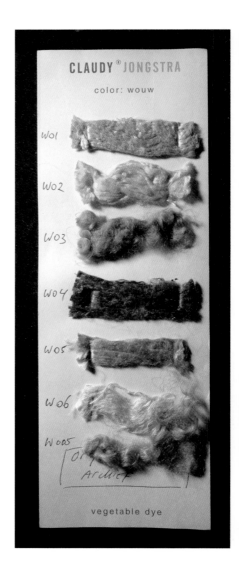

Colour Swatches

The effect of Indigo on different kinds of wool

Blues

English name	Indigo
Dutch name	Indigo
Family	Fabaceae
Genus	Indigofera
Species	Indigofera tinctoria
Origin	India

The most important indigotin-bearing plants are:
- Indigofera tinctoria (Asia, Central and South America)
- Polygonum tinctorium (China and Japan)
- Lonchocaropus cyanescenos (Africa)
- Isatis tinctoria (Europe)

The indigo shrub is one of more than 600 species in the Indigofera genus. It is a plant from the extensive family of Fabaceae, the papilionaceous legumes. The shrub has small leaflets and butterfly-like flowers composed of five parts. The indigo shrub grows to a height between 1 and 2 metres and originates from India, from where it has been dispersed around the globe. The different species of the Indigofera genus are primarily found in tropical and subtropical regions.

The shrub has been in use as a source of dye for at least 5,000 years. The pigment's precursor, indican, is extracted from the leaves and stems by crushing them finely and mixing the pulp with water. The concoction is colourless at this point, but when left to ferment for half a day it reacts with the surrounding air and the oxidation process converts it into indigotin, the blue pigment. The reaction can be accelerated by stirring the water at regular intervals.

110. Isatis tinctoria L.
Woad; Y.

Reds/Pinks

English name	Cochineal
Dutch name	Cochenilleluis
Family	Dactylopiidae
Genus	Dactylopius
Species	Coccus
Origin	pre-Hispanic Mexico

The pigment cochineal, or carmine red, is extracted from three different species of scale insects: the kermes louse from Europe, and the Polish and American cochineal shield-louse. Only the female insects are used in the production of the dye. Variations in colour can arise depending on the type of insect used and the production method. For example, the kermes louse indigenous to Europe yields a lighter shade of dye than the American cochineal louse.

The Egyptians, Greeks and Romans already used the pigment of the kermes louse to dye wool, leather and silk in ancient times. The colour of the pigment was known as carmine or scarlet red. Use of the European kermes louse swiftly declined after the discovery of the American cochineal bug, since the latter was more productive, providing a higher yield of dyestuff. From 1554, the Spanish imported insects from South America in great quantity, so from that time the lice could also be cultivated in certain parts of Europe.

The American cochineal insect is a white-coloured louse found on the pads of Opuntia cacti. It lives there as a parasite and feeds from the sap of the cactus. The pigment is extracted from the blood of the shield-louse and above all from its eggs, so the lice are collected and killed just before laying their eggs offspring. Then they are dried, crushed and filtered. At this stage the product is not yet a colourfast pigment, which is achieved by adding tin or alum to the dyestuff.

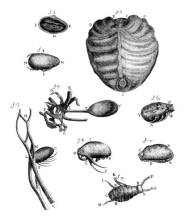

Colour Swatches

The effect of Cochineal on different kinds of wool.

Colour Swatches

The effect of Walnut on different kinds of wool.

Browns

English name	Walnut
Dutch name	Walnoot
Origin	Eastern North America (Black Walnut), Persia (Persian Walnut)
Family	Juglandaceae
Genus	Juglans
Species	Nigra (Black Walnut)
Species	Regia (Persian Walnut)

A brown dye is made from the leaves, bark and husks of the walnut tree. The intensity of the colour depends on the variety of walnut and its maturity when harvested.

raw silk / Merino wool / silk organza

raw silk / Drenthe Heath / Merino wool / silk chiffon

raw silk / Drenthe Heath / Merino wool / Alpaca

raw silk / Merino wool / silk chiffon

Drenthe Heath / Merino wool / silk chiffon

Merino wool / silk metallic organza

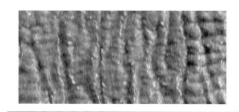

raw silk / Drenthe Heath / Wensleydale wool /
Merino wool / silk chiffon

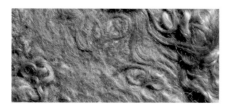

raw silk / silk chiffon

raw silk / Merino wool / silk chiffon

raw silk / Merino wool / silk organza / raw linen *

Merino wool / silk organza / silk chiffon

raw silk / Drenthe Heath / Merino wool / silk chiffon

raw silk / Drenthe Heath / Wensleydale wool / Merino wool

raw silk / Wensleydale wool / Merino wool / silk chiffon

raw silk / Wensleydale wool / Merino wool / silk chiffon

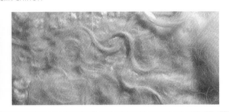

raw silk / Drenthe Heath / Wensleydale wool / Merino wool / silk chiffon

raw silk / cotton gauze / Merino wool / silk chiffon

raw silk / Wensleydale wool / Merino wool / silk chiffon

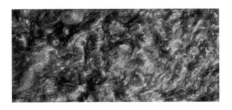

raw šilk / Drenthe Heath / cotton gauze

Drenthe Heath / yak / Merino wool / silk chiffon

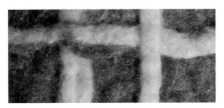

"My way of working is the product of a moral aversion to the fashion industry. Different collections have to be sold and consumed every year. This excess of fabric means that people never wear their clothes out any more. Besides, production is so speeded up that it is impossible to supply quality. After my graduation, I saw an exhibition on the process of producing felt in the Tilburg Textile Museum. I was amazed: that wool, the oldest material in the world, has so many specific qualities! Industrial, synthetic materials are no match for it.

Since then quality has meant sustainability for me. I sell you a piece of material for the rest of your life – also because there is a certain timelessness in the design, with historical, natural colours and structures that lead you into the forgotten world of our heritage. One of my felt walls in a hypermodern office building yields an experience that you can usually only find in museums today. It is often a confusing experience, because people no longer know what untreated wool feels like.

The idea of timelessness also determines my work process. I control every link in that chain, from the sheep to the herb garden for the dye. I increase the scale by going deeper. I have always been thirsty for knowledge. My own empirical research and scientific research in collaboration with, for example, TNO and the Instituut Collectie Nederland are a part of my way of working. So I turned down a request to go and give a crash course in felt production in Mongolia. My vision calls for a structural approach, a plan involving many years.

Sustainability implies not only a craftsmanlike way of working but above all also working with materials direct from the ground, which are down-to-earth in the most direct sense of the word. If you do that, people will start to become concerned about the earth as well. And that is what I eventually want in my work: to appeal to people's ecological awareness. Handicraft is for me a tool, not an end in itself. I hesitated for a long time as to whether I should study law. It has become 'doing justice to the physical earth'."

Projects
2002-2009

Product	carpet
Material	raw silk, Drenthe Heath, Wensleydale and Merino wool, cotton gauze
Location	Rotterdam, the Netherlands

Product   wall coverings
Material   raw silk, Merino wool, silk metallic organza
Location   Utrecht, the Netherlands

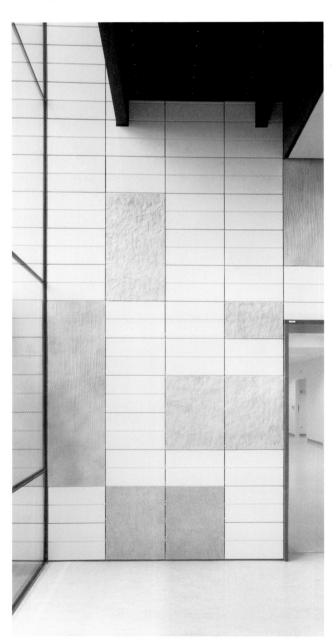

Lloyd Hotel and Cultural Embassy

Architect   MVRDV
Product   window blinds
Material   Merino wool, raw silk, cotton gauze, Alpaca
Location   Amsterdam, the Netherlands

Restaurant Kunsthal

Architect	OMA
Product	wall coverings
Material	yak hair, Drenthe Heath, Merino wool, cotton gauze
Location	Rotterdam, the Netherlands

University Medical Centre

Project   art installation
Material   Merino wool, raw silk, guipure technique, silk chiffon
Location   Utrecht, the Netherlands

Project	multifunctional room
Architect	Claus en Kaan Architects
Product	wall hangings
Material	raw silk, Merino wool, silk chiffon
Location	Nijverdal, the Netherlands

Project	council chamber exterior
Architect	Claus en Kaan Architects
Product	wall coverings
Material	raw silk, Merino wool, silk chiffon
Location	Nijverdal, the Netherlands

House of Culture and Government

Project	theatre
Architect	Claus en Kaan Architects
Product	wall coverings
Material	raw silk, Merino wool, silk chiffon
Location	Nijverdal, the Netherlands

Entry Hall Triodos Bank

Project   art installation
Material   Drenthe Heath, raw silk, Merino wool, silk organza
Location   Zeist, the Netherlands

Architect	Jo Coenen
Product	wall coverings
Material	Drenthe Heath, Wensleydale wool, raw silk, Merino wool, chiffon
Location	Amsterdam, the Netherlands

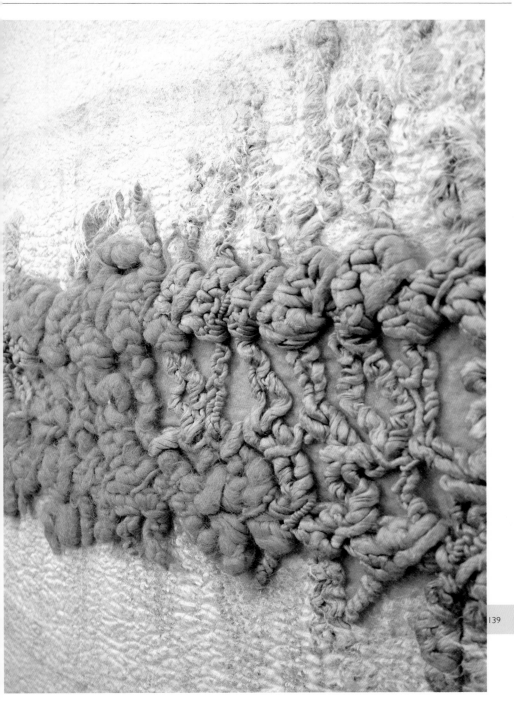

Project   art installation
Material   raw silk, Merino wool, silk chiffon, silk metal organza, silk organza, raw linen
Location   Almelo, the Netherlands

Dollhouse of Petronella Oortmans

Project   art commission for Dollhouse of Petronella Oortmans
Material   Merino wool, raw silk, silk chiffon
Location   Rijksmuseum, Amsterdam, the Netherlands

De Pont

Project   art installation, in collaboration with Marc Mulders
Material   Drenthe Heath, Wensleydale wool, raw silk, silk chiffon, Merino wool
Location   De Pont, Museum of Contemporary Art, Tilburg, the Netherlands

Private Residence

Project wall hanging
Material Drenthe Heath, Merino wool, raw silk, silk organza
Location 's-Hertogenbosch, the Netherlands

Project   art installation
Material   Drenthe Heath, Wensleydale and Merino wool, raw silk, silk chiffon
Location   Cooper Hewitt, National Design Museum, New York, USA

Onix

Onix

The Onix architecture office was established by Alex van de Beld (b. 1963) and Haiko Meijer (b. 1961) in 1994. All their projects display a fascination for materials, construction, detail, location, improvisation and a contemporary interpretation of traditional techniques. The firm also formulates theoretical propositions and reflects on its own architectural practices by writing manifestos. For Onix, the quest to discover the appropriate form and structure involves the contribution of users and builders. Moreover, a building only acquires a clear-cut significance during its construction and in its actual use. The factors of time, coincidence and improvisation are essential to the design process. Building by trial and error has actually been elevated to the guiding principle for Onix's temporarily onsite installations. It represents one means of positively channelling an aversion to over-regulation and uniformity in Dutch architecture, and of taking best advantage of site-specific qualities. For many years the firm has been experimenting with the typology of barns, a structural form that presents numerous freedoms while evoking a sense of trusted familiarity, since the barn is an archetype in our collective memory. Falling into the trap of an overly literal proclivity for the historical is avoided by intensifying the contrast between the familiar and the alienating.

Dirty Regionalism

The Perfect Imperfection of Onix Architects
— by Roemer van Toorn

Exclusive Authenticity

The air is heavy with the desire for authentic experiences. We've had enough
of the standardised products that the world of commerce offers us. "Cook your
own shoes! Dream and spice it up as you please. This is your art and your inven-
tion" - that's the Puma "Mongolian Shoe BBQ" website.[1] Puma cleverly responds
to the demand for exclusive authenticity. On the web, you can enjoy yourself
sitting at a rather worn wooden table in a picturesque restaurant, and with the
assistance of a handsome maître chef from Mongolia you can put together your
own exclusive Puma shoes from a buffet of thirty different kinds of materials,
colours, textures and types of leather. The personal touch and involvement have
now come to join brand name and extravagant price as components of the cult
of exclusiveness. You no longer go to a shop to buy something — as in the anon-
ymous supermarket — but you set out in search of personal, authentic experiences. We want to be waited on, preferably by skilled and elegant specialists who
are capable of tracing the very best in the archives of history, an exquisite wine
region or an outstanding design academy. It's like classical music — you prefer
not to play on synthetic strings. There's nothing above hearing the sigh of the
natural string made of catgut. When the musician plays it at its best, the instrument should suffer.

Mass demonstrations against disaster capitalism are difficult nowadays.[2] We
prefer to stay closer to home. We buy Max Havelaar fair trade coffee to enjoy
an aromatic, politically correct cup at home. We'd rather savour biological, exotic fast-food soups produced by Michel Jansen's De Kleinste Soepfabriek in the
Groningen countryside.[3] We've set out on the road of Practical Idealism as for-
mulated by Natasja van der Berg and Sophie Koers.[4] We savour slow food, we
buy products from the honest shopping list, we follow know what you eat, we
wear hip and honest clothing, we help the cow into the meadow, use the car
now and then, and give to charity once in a while. In short, you assume responsibility for your actions and their effect on the world around you without feeling guilty that you're doing something non-idealist. And the Like-a-local website
guarantees authentic and exclusive experiences for this upper middle class when

151

it is travelling: "Live in unique places; from a houseboat in Amsterdam to a loft in Barcelona."[5] Strolling through Amsterdam becomes an interactive journey past local galleries, special fashion and design stores like The Frozen Fountain,[6] Droog Design,[7] and the Paul Année bakery with its homemade unleavened bread with onion conserve and authentic French rye bread.

It's not just the quality of the product that counts; where it has come from, whether it has been produced in an environment-friendly, non-industrial way, the personal, creative story behind the product and how quality has been achieved during the process all play a decisive role too.

In fact, in every field there is an increasing emphasis on the sensual,[8] on personal and creative stimuli, attention for yourself, friendship, a sense of community, and caring about the environment. The lack of personal identity, the loss of long-term experiences and the fear of the unfamiliar in our global world not only inspire the upper middle class, commercial enterprises and religions, but they also arouse the romantic and sentimental nostalgia for what is local in the arts, design and architecture. While religious fundamentalists minimise every form of globalisation and adhere to the *Blut und Boden* of a region, it is precisely the global that many inspiring designers, artists and architects fail to repudiate in their concentration on what is authentic in a region. Glocal Regionalists would be a good term for them.[9] The local and the universal aspects of our global culture are brought into relation with one another in surprising and paradoxical ways. For instance, at the invitation of Puma, Marcel Wanders transformed the international style of the notorious white plastic party tent that you can buy in any DIY store.[10] The white tent was made lower, attractively decorated, and accompanied by all kinds of travel and picnic accessories under the name "A collection for those who hate camping." Wanders' subversive design intervention transforms the universal roof of the camp-site party tent into a lounge location for creative picnic activities in urban areas.

Playing with the new world under the influence of globalisation, standardisation and commerce alone is not enough for the architects, artists and designers – among whom I include Wanders – who practise glocal regionalism. They are tired of the datamania of the famous Superdutch architects who charted the universal standardisation and metropolitanism of our global culture industry.[11] Traditions, direct interaction with users, craftsmanship, sustainable and pure – preferably ecological – materials are rated higher by this new movement of designers, artists and architects in the Netherlands. They exploit the potential resistance that lies in the shock-proof, recalcitrant and asymmetrical qualities of the local to brake the homogenising force of the global. The question, however, is whether the present predilection for the local, in perverse collusion with the global, really is able to offer an alternative to the quasi-authenticity that the Wanders-Puma duo and others are developing. In other words, given the paradoxical condition of glocal regionalism, to what extent is it possible to develop a progressive alternative to the shock therapy of disaster capitalism?[12]

This is not the first time that architects are appealing to the individual, authentic and sustainable qualities of a region. By way of general definition, Alex Tzonis and Liane Lefaivre already commented on regionalism in 1981 that it "upholds the individual and local architectonic features against more universal and abstract ones."[13] Kenneth Frampton, Alexander Tzonis, Liane Lefaivre – following Lewis Mumford[14] – launched the concept of Critical Regionalism to counter the placelessness and lack of meaning in Modern Architecture by using contextual forces. Frampton put forth his views in his essay "Towards a Critical Regionalism: Six points of an architecture of resistance."[15] He evokes Paul Ricoeur's question of "how to become modern and to return to sources; how to revive an old, dormant civilization and take part in universal civilization." According to Frampton, Critical Regionalism should adopt modern architecture critically for its universal progressive qualities, but at the same time should value responses that are specific to the context. The emphasis is on topography, climate, light and tectonic form instead of scenography, and on tactile rather than visual qualities. However much we might welcome Critical Regionalism's search for social alternatives, I don't think that it goes far enough. In applying the concept of Critical Regionalism to the current practice of the Onix firm of architects, we shall discover that, on the one hand, Critical Regionalism has a limited conception of the local and of how the architectural object works. On the other hand, Critical Regionalism forgets time and again to indicate how architecture can function democratically. In fact, this article raises the question of to what extent the renewed interest in and physical appearance of the local, as a form of discovering authenticity under the influence of the global, may offer a shock-proof and more universal form of resistance than Critical Regionalism can ever provide. Unlike Critical Regionalism, Dirty Regionalism embraces the dirtiness of everyday life, with all the risks that that entails. It is in the dirtiness of the glocal – and not in the élitist and essentialist perfection of the local, where Critical Regionalism situates it – that Dirty Regionalism seeks its opposition and alternatives to the lack of meaning under the influence of commercialisation, standardisation and globalisation. Drawing on the work of Onix, I shall discuss the five main principles of this Dirty Regionalism.[16]

1.   Dirty hands

The Dogma manifesto "The Vow of Chastity" (1995) was an attack on the sclerosis and decadence of commercial cinema by the film directors Lars von Trier, Thomas Vinterberg and other important members of the group. They had had enough of corrupt illusionism, the arsenal of technical tricks and sentimentality in film. Dogma 95 challenged the dominance of Hollywood on the basis of its loss of authenticity and whom it represented. The Onix architects cleverly profile themselves by writing a similar Dogma manifesto for architecture, and they are also opposed to the star architecture of such Hollywood architects as Frank Gehry, Rob Krier, Sjoerd Soeters and the many different kinds of commercial architecture. Since manifestos of this kind are rare, it is worthwhile to cite the dos and don'ts of the Onix Dogma: "(1) The design is made specifically for the location. (2) Façades are never designed independently of ground plans and vice versa. (3) Drawings and models are made by hand. (4) Materials are used in their natural state. (5) Illustrations in drawings and reference images are prohibited. (6) The building should not contain any referential or unnecessary ornaments. (7) Architecture takes place here and now. (8) All drawings are done by the architect. (9) Stylised designs are not accepted. (10) The architect is not referred to as such."

And what goes for Dogma 95 applies to Onix as well: "I swear as a director from personal taste. I am no longer an artist, I swear to refrain from creating a 'work', as I regard the instant as more important than the whole. My supreme goal is to force the truth out of my characters and settings. I swear to do so by all the means available and at the cost of my good taste and any aesthetic considerations."[17] The Dogma of Onix and the Danish film directors does not really operate on the basis of the need for social criticism. They do not implement political projects to criticise the middle class or the status quo, or to champion the oppressed. Any commentary on the status quo is a chance side-effect. Onix is concerned with authentic expressions and actions that go beyond hypnotic representations. They are interested in experiential diversity in space, in a location as a form of social action. Unlike Critical Regionalism, that mainly presents intact, tidy Modernist buildings, Onix opts for rough, unfinished materials. Their buildings are just as unfinished, grubby and dirty as the handheld camera shots that Vinterberg used in *Celebration*, or Von Trier's shots of the countryside in *The Idiots*. Vinterberg and Von Trier turn the viewer into an almost pornographic voyeur. They use the subversive dirt of our society to hold a looking-glass to us – we recognise our own perversion and secretly feel at home in it – while at the same time we perceive through it the possibility of a different world. Instead of turning their backs on the cliché as the Critical Regionalists do, Von Trier, Vinterberg and Onix make clever use of the cliché in their quest for social authenticity. In other words, the dirt of society harbours a critical potential, not as an independent factor, but as a communicational instrument to be deployed in the striving for emancipation. While the Critical Regionalists sterilise the everyday by absorbing all local influences in the autonomy and abstraction of tectonics,[18] Onix is prepared to run risks in embracing the popular, the folkloric, even the cardboard qualities of the everyday. Onix has no qualms about imperfection or the taste of others. Onix is prepared to dirty its hands in its negotiation with the users, the sub-contractor, the situation on location and vernacular traditions. Instead of isolating itself in the sterile world of art for art's sake, Onix endeavours to relate to the reality around us which is just getting dirtier and dirtier. It is precisely by embracing what is conventional – the typology of the farm, the sentiments of the users and complex economic limiting conditions – that Onix is able to communicate with the local setting and its users, while at the same time the unprecedented rough and imperfect tectonics opens up new worlds of use. The road that Onix has chosen is by no means an easy one. All kinds of cultural and social meanings are suddenly at stake that go beyond the architectural profession. It's no longer possible to steer a course blindly following the automatic dictates of architecture. What counts is to take notice of what gives direction to the profession outside its own discourse. It is not for nothing that Onix is keen to take the actual architectural experiences of users and visitors into account and to build installations together with local users and architects.

2.   From representation to information

Critical Regionalism and Dirty Regionalism do not comment on the status quo; they both offer an alternative to it. Critical Regionalism's alternative clings to the representative expression of architectural tectonics; how the construction, its principle of cladding and thereby the details of a building can embody durable values. The starting point is not so much the (changeable) programme of life as what can be (permanently) incorporated in the disciplinary practice of the profession. A rolling mountain landscape can be beautifully picked up in the roofscape of a building. As for the interaction of the user, how a construction generates complex narratives is not the strongest point of Critical Regionalism. Critical Regionalism adheres to essential binary oppositions. It manifests itself against the visual and for the tactile, against the space and for the place, against the city and for the countryside. While Critical Regionalism is exclusive, Dirty Regionalism opts for a hybrid approach: both urban and rural, both natural

155

and artificial, both visual and tactile, both beautiful and ugly, both smooth and rough, and so on. Critical Regionalism puts its trust in the permanent aspects of architecture. Critical Regionalists forget that our experience and the life of things are much more complex than they would have us believe. And that complexity is only increasing under the influence of the global culture industry.[19] Our relation to objects in our global culture long ago became a dynamic instead of a static one. Cultural identities assumed a dynamic form of their own in our culture of circulation; value is added in the movement. The effect of an object on social subjects is no longer determined from above as it was in the era of Theodor Adorno,[20] but is subject to the constant differences and multiplicity that the global cultural industry produces. We are the ones who put together our exclusive Puma shoes. It is no longer a single panoptic centre that is in control, but the active participation of every individual in the economic process. It is not for nothing that the Onix book maNUfesto for an authentic experience of architecture is entitled Awaiting Signification.[21] The experience of the user is the main factor for Onix. Their book Awaiting Signification searches for "the illuminating spots where the everyday forces its way in, where there is also place for exception and resistance; spots where academic autism is riddled by the rhizome of authenticity." Onix are not after a representative final image, but a result that is interactive and geared to change. It is not for nothing that Zwolle residents are invited to plot their own routes through the Exodus building. The imperfections and uncertainties of life are an important ingredient in the work of Onix. A construction must have an interactive capacity. Critical Regionalism hopes to confer identity on people with its static tectonics, while the Dirty Regionalism of Onix creates authentic moments by the production of difference. Onix are out to establish relations between things – what the performance of a building can mean to the viewer and the user. Seen in operational terms, Critical Regionalism is representative of origin, while Dirty Regionalism is informative by nature. Dirty Regionalism is dirty because it embraces the logic of the global cultural industry. While Critical Regionalism is concerned with the industrial, agricultural and cultural processing of raw materials, the global cultural industry is not focused on the primary quality of materials but on a culture of the constant exchange of meanings based on a collective ideal of sharing. The work does not set out to manipulate references or to cite, but it redefines notions of creation, authorship and originality through the use of cultural artefacts. The materials that they use are a part of our global cultural industry. The work has script-like qualities. The screenplay becomes form. "It is no longer a matter of elaborating a form on the basis of a raw material", Nicolas Bourriaud writes, "but working with objects that are already in circulation on the cultural market, which is to say, objects already informed by other objects and subjects. Notions of originality (being at the origin of) and even of creation (making something from nothing) are slowly blurred in this new cultural landscape marked by the twin figures of the DJ and the programmer, both of whom have the task of selecting cultural objects and inserting them into new contexts."[22] Through its method of postproduction, Dirty Regionalism explicitly positions itself vis-à-vis our mass culture, which is full of Dirty Realism. Retreating into the academy, or withdrawing into an élitist and usually expensive tacky (Western) home with Critical Regionalist allure are not the answer. The benchmark is not the genius loci or its embodiment, but the narrative of the construction – in other words, what Onix call the scenius loci can be activated by involving the user in the project.

3.   Unfamiliar familiarity

In the theatre of Bertold Brecht, the audience is constantly reminded that the actor is both a fictive character and a flesh-and-blood actor. Such a consciousness creates critical distance while you remain a part of everyday reality. You suddenly perceive what you belong to, what its principles are, what is problematic and where the openings lie. So it is not a question of the one or the other, but of the qualitative linking of the unfamiliar and the familiar. The dialectical conjunction of universal principles and local values makes a work interesting. Thus the Onnen Villa, the island farm (ecological care farm) in Noordlaren, and the DogmA house – all by Onix – skilfully combine the idea of the continuous space with the typology of a folkloristic farmhouse. Alienation as method is a problematical principle for Critical Regionalism; it is primarily about homecoming and reconciliation after a hectic working day in the bustle of the city. Onix do not determine the identity of the homecoming; the experience of climate, natural surroundings, material, light and landscape in an ecologically sound climate is not all that counts. It is precisely the absurd contradictions too that can make the experience of homecoming so rich. The car, asphalt or folklore need not damage the idea of homecoming – as Frampton supposes – but they can in fact widen one's view.[23] The DogmA house, for instance, is both a picturesque little home and an inviting collective roof. For Onix, alienation only takes on meaning in an ambiguous relation with the familiar. This is not to produce creative and aesthetically attractive shock effects, but to gradually allow familiar worlds to grow accustomed to alienation. Onix immunises familiar worlds by confronting them with the unfamiliar.

4.   Dirty Details

Authenticity is not a static concept – something of the tectonics itself – in Dirty Regionalism, but it comes to life through activity, once the users occupy the building by being active. This form of authenticity is activated by a smaller or larger degree of inconsistency in the whole. Like the Japanese principle of Wabi-sabi, something does not become authentic until it satisfies three simple realities: nothing has eternal life, nothing is complete, and nothing is perfect. Perfection lies in imperfection. Such Dirty Details take into account the programmatic and cultural narratives that a detail manages to communicate through its technical and aesthetic discourses. Sometimes the very material that Onix deploys is dirty. Literally dirty, as rough as sandpaper. They are down-to-earth materials, weathered or unpainted wood that changes colour in the sunlight and intensely stimulates the senses. Is it a house or a barn? From a distance it looks so completely wooden, unfinished in both senses of the word. Sometimes Onix deploys stronger generators of difference, such as a continuous floor that finds its way to the roof. Besides offering shade and a sense of security, the roof invites the user to possess it. It is as though the street blends into the roof and becomes a square. It enables the residents to enjoy drifting in from outdoors as in the DogmA house. It is the forms and the material that interrupt, agitate, and sometimes even insinuate. The presentation of the Onix Dogma manifesto was accompanied by a pack of sanding paper. Material is allowed to be dirty, unpolished, imperfect, fragile, urban and extreme.

While Critical Regionalism encounters the region, digs it up and strips it of its scenographic bad taste, Dirty Regionalism reinvents it through the schizophrenic condition of the global society. For Dirty Regionalism the global society is also capable of developing potential differences that generate freedom. Freedom is produced not only in the dialectical difference between the local aspect of traditional societies and the universal. Not just the earthscape, the roofscape, the local climate, the topography, or local materials can have an emancipatory effect, but global influences – those of our mass, reflexive culture – can have one too. [24]

It is the dirt of the earth that has an inspiring effect. With an adherence to a preindustrial idea of ground, Mondrian's and Van Doesburg's movement De Stijl could never have emerged. Their abstract colours, fields, lines and patterns may not literally be found in the landscape of the Netherlands, but they are certainly determined by the Dutch cultural landscape. What is authentic is not finding a craft, traditional or particular material, but what its deployment generates for use. While the craft or material of a potato crate is fairly crude, as perfect imperfection it can fulfil its purpose if you take into account the collective memory of a site and know what it has to target. In East Groningen, Onix designed a crate house made of materials from the immediate surroundings that had been used before. The crate house consists of 4,000 stacked crates with the smell of potatoes from a distant past. This collection of dirty crates transformed into a resting point in the landscape embodies the social history of a largely erased past. These Dirty Details, referring to potato cultivation in Groningen, reflect for a moment on a landscape that was completely different in the past, before the idyllic reforestation had permanently eradicated every historic trace of the agrarian landscape.

5. "We make the road by walking"

In 1987 Paulo Freire invited his colleague Myles Horton to engage in a dialogue about education as an emancipatory practice.[25] Freire asks: "Is it possible to discuss, to study the phenomenon of life without discussing exploitation, domination, freedom, democracy, and so on?" They are in agreement that the answer is no; they reject the idea of neutrality in education. According to Freire, what matters is not having an opinion, but the sharing of ideas in such a way that more room is created for the students to disagree, so that they can find their own way in a better understanding of things. Freire and Horton create a space in which everyone comes to a richer insight into the topic under discussion on the basis of disagreement. In other words, disagreeing, saying what is at stake, and coming into collision helps you to find your way. It is precisely the jolts – the dirt on the road – that point the way. With *Awaiting Signification* in the Exodus project and the "doG manifesto (a non-contemporary pilgrimage in 10 paths)", Onix opts for the same educational approach as Freire and Horton. Their list of assignments for ten spaces in *Awaiting Signification* challenges the visitors to discover them for themselves. "Space 1 Walk around the building before you enter it. Space 2 Sketch the building. Space 3 Find a way through the building by getting lost. […] Space 8 Smell, feel, see, listen and taste the building. Space 9 Meet other people in the building. Space 10 Be receptive to the experience of another." "doG a non-contemporary pilgrimage in 10 paths" is an attempt to indicate 10 directions in which various installations can be built on location in collaboration with local architects and users.[26] So the beauty of a building by Onix lies not in its overall appearance nor in its utility – only through the road you make by walking through the building and how you produce it together. Or in the words of Onix: "It is not a question of restoring the true relation between the tectonic and the a-tectonic, or of revising the relation between the functional and the poetic. It is about building on what is said about it, because that is connected with how it is used and experienced."[27] Onix is thereby stating that architecture is by definition ambiguous and enigmatic, an endless work in which a story arises from several stories, detached and intertwined, in a hermetic openness. Critical Regionalism, on the other hand, adopts a position based on a single authority: that of the architect and his (Western) profession.

Democratic Design

As we have seen in the introduction to this article and in the work of Onix, the importance of the authentic and the desire for exclusiveness can assume many guises. Puma also jumps onto the desire for exclusive authenticity bandwagon. When Onix invites visitors to enter the Exodus building with Captain Beefheart Revisited music on the iPod, this "dirty" approach seems to have a lot in common with the quasi-authenticity of subversive commerce. Both the work of Onix and that of subversive commerce derive the strength of a work from the differences that it can generate in dialogue with the viewer and user. The meditative moment arises through the lack of an all too direct and fluid conjunction between the different worlds that are brought together in the design. It is as though there is a gap, a void, between the one and the other that causes agitation and invites you to complete the work. What distinguishes the designers in the exhibition *Tangible Traces* from the world of commerce is that their dirty conjunctions have a highly specific goal in mind. They join Frampton and myself in asking: "How exactly do we reenergize and reactivate the design professions and, above all, our digitalized, consumer society, politically speaking, given the way it is currently sequestered by the triumph of globalization? How do we recover the references we have lost or are in process of losing?"[28] While Frampton opts for a double critique, a strategy of tactile elements as opposed to the visual, and of tectonic elements as opposed to the stenographic – i.e. a distanced, unimpaired identity – Dirty Regionalism focuses on how the field of tension between the differences can steer emancipation. What Onix brings out in its work is that the desire for the authentic along the lines of the cleansing rules of Critical Regionalism does not work politically at all. Critical regionalism confines itself to the tectonics of architecture instead of investigating how spatial constructions generate democratic narratives. Critical Regionalism does not like the unexpected, the uncertain, difference and unfamiliarity. It prefers answers to uncertain and open constructions.

In this respect Critical Regionalism resembles the police. Unlike politicians, the police want to normalise everything that is subversive or revolutionary as quickly as possible. Uncertainty is what the police always want to combat, while politics is a question of fertile disagreements that keep on inspiring reflection and further emancipation in conflict with the status quo. It is therefore hardly surprising that the Critical Regionalists have never issued pronouncements on the city. Unlike Dirty Regionalists, Critical Regionalists lack a cosmopolitan vision. Under the provocative title of Dirty Regionalism, I have tried to chart a technique of stoppages, gaps and assemblages that, with its intrinsic critical capacity, emancipates the idea of a wall, roof or type in relation to the "choreography" of use.[29] Like the political scientist Chantal Mouffe, I am searching for democratic designs "which would provide the basis for a vibrant agonistic (as opposed to antagonistic) debate as to the shape and the future of the common life."[30] I am convinced that the Dirty Regionalism of Onix is on the right track towards an agonistic space by means of their perfect imperfection.

NOTES

1   www.mongolianshoebbq.puma.com or via the website www.puma.com

2   Naomi Klein, *The Shock Doctrine. The Rise of Disaster Capitalism*, 2007.

3   www.kleinstesoepfabriek.nl The concept is a tasty soup – a French cauliflower soup or an exotic apricot and carrot soup – evoking a trip abroad that tastes surprisingly different every time by standardising the production as little as possible.

4   See their *Praktisch Idealisme. Handboek voor de beginnende wereldverbeteraar* (2003) and *Fairshopping* (2004) or their internet site: www.praktischidealisme.nl/portaaltje
Bill Clinton's recent *Giving. How each of us can change the world* (2007) belongs to the same ideology of Practical Idealism, witness his statement: "Almost everyone [...] can do something useful for others, and in the process, strengthen the fabric of our shared humanity."
See www.clintonfoundation.org

5   www.Like-a-Local.com "Meet a local and be surprised by their secret addresses in the city. Dine with a local at their home, taste and experience the local atmosphere."

6   www.frozenfountain.nl The Frozen Fountain, beside the Prinsengracht in Amsterdam, is a shop/gallery that sells contemporary furniture and home accessories. The Frozen Fountain maintains close contacts with designers from the various art academies in the Netherlands and elsewhere, so that a dynamic collection comes into being as a result.

7   www.droogdesign.nl Droog Design has its headquarters in a splendid historic building dating from 1641, Staalstraat 7a/7b, in the centre of Amsterdam. The 300 m² space on the ground floor was designed by the Müller and Van Tol studios. The space is divided into a shop, furnished with products from the Droog collection which can be purchased on the spot, and a gallery space where new work by young talented designers is exhibited every two months.

8   See too the 52nd Venice Biennale, *Think with the Senses – Feel with the Mind*, 2007.

9   Sociologists use the term Glocal (= Local + Global) to indicate that the local cannot exist without the global and vice versa.

10 www.marcelwanders.com and www.wanders.
    puma.com "I hate camping. But I love lounging in
    Style. Outdoor living usually conjures images of
    campsites, hot dogs and over-stuffed backpacks.
    Why should design and fashion be limited to city
    living?"

11 Bart Lootsma, *Superdutch. New Architecture in the
    Netherlands*, Princeton Architectural Press, New
    York, 2000.

12 See note 2 (Naomi Klein)

13 Alexander Tzonis and Liane Lefaivre, "The grid
    and the pathway. An introduction to the work of
    Dimitris and Susana Antonakakis", *Architecture in
    Greece* 15, Athens, 1981.

14 Vincent B. Canizaro (ed.), *Architectural
    Regionalism. Collective writings on Place, Identity,
    Modernity and Tradition*, Princeton Architectural
    Press, New York, 2007.

15 Kenneth Frampton, "Towards a Critical
    Regionalism: Six Points for an Architecture of
    Resistance", in Hal Foster (ed.), *The Anti-Aesthetic.
    Essays on Postmodern Culture*, Bay Press, Port
    Townsend, 1983.

16 Dirty Regionalism is not a condition but a posi-
    tion. I thereby exclude a condition whereby all
    kinds of local practices such as rickshaws and the
    Thai TukTuk (www.tuctuktuk.nl/site/tuctuktuk.
    php) are imported into the West as quasi-authen-
    tic identity gadgets. A Dirty Regionalism of this
    kind is at home in the condition of dirty realism,
    i.e. perverse glocal conditions in which the local
    cannot be divorced from the glocal and the global
    cannot function without the local.

17 Dogma 95 manifesto as quoted in the article
    "Dogma 95" by John Roberts in *New Left Review*,
    no. 238, 1999.

18 Local influences are such factors as the topogra-
    phy (roofscape, earthwork), climate, light, material

and craftsmanship.

19 See too Scott Lash and Celia Lury, *Global
    Culture Industry. The Mediation of Things*, Polity,
    Cambridge, 2005.

20 See Theodor Adorno, *The Culture Industry.
    Selected Essays on Mass Culture*, Routledge,
    London, 2001 and Max Horkheimer and Adorno,
    Dialectic of Enlightenment (1944), Continuum, New
    York, 1973.

21 Onix, *Awaiting Signification. MaNUfesto for an au-
    thentic experience of architecture,* NAi Publishers,
    Rotterdam, 2005.

22 Nicolas Bourriaud, *Postproduction*, Lukas &
    Sternberg, New York, 2007.

23 See too the unimplemented Onix design for an
    interior showroom in Leek.

24 We even find new forms of communality on inter-
    net – the virtual reality par excellence. See www.
    facebook.com or www.couchsurfing.com

25 Myles Horton and Paulo Freire, *We Make the
    Road by Walking: Conversations on Education
    and Social Change*, Temple University Press,
    Philadelphia, 1990.

26 "Path 1 NOWthentic, is each time a new road that
    ends in a mimesis of the authentic. Path 2 Scenius
    Loci, is trodden together by local parties and out-
    siders. […] Path 8 Unfamiliar familiarity, convention
    is illuminated through emancipation", 2007.

27 See note 21 (Onix).

28 Kenneth Frampton in 'Postscript to "Critical
    Regionalism Revisited": A Response to Mark
    Gilbert and Bart Lootsma' at www.agglutinations.
    com/archives, 10 November 2003.

29 It is the democratic space of the visual, physi-
    cal and non-verbal, the space of the body and of
    (ritual) procedures.

30 Chantal Mouffe, *The Return of the Political.
    Thinking in Action*, Routledge, London, 2005.

"Everything is standardised in our society today. Markets, budgets, behaviour and certainly the image as well. We try to handle these aspects in a different way. As far as the image is concerned, for example, we create something that is recognisable and contemporary, but which nevertheless also has a connection with history – something that forms part of our visual culture, but at the same time escapes from it and evokes a strange familiarity. We like to proceed on the basis of a kind of primal intuition, of concepts from a distant past that everyone knows, such as a hut, a cave, a megalithic tomb. The next step is to come up with our interpretation of them.

For instance, we also deploy the archetype of the shed. In abstraction, our sheds are functional spaces that challenge the user to put them to a different use. Like our installations, they provoke interaction with the person who lives there. Compare it with Onix. With this spelling, our name evokes not only the material onyx but other meanings too.

Quality for us is emphatically the design of a quality *environment*. The projects that we do are never isolated from their context. We do not design a house, but a house in dialogue with the location. Both the spatial quality and the feeling of the surroundings have to be involved. Intelligent fitting in is not enough. The building must issue an appeal to the environment. A schoolyard can be a closed area for children at play, but it can also be a centre of hospitality in the neighbourhood.

The reinterpretation of handicraft techniques, often deploying present-day techniques, is always important in that process. A beautiful old biddle joint adds layers to a building. The user feels that it has been made lovingly. Architecture that is only designed on the basis of form, without interaction with the material, is artificial and empty. Moreover, by leaving room for improvisation, as every craftsman does, we do not rule out unforeseen options. We call it 'design as you build'. In the culture of the present there is no longer any room for the factors of time and uncertainty, even though they are precisely what you have to deal with in practice. Taking the time to try things out: it is a sensibility that we use and which makes us aware that we want to be a practice that is not contemporary."

Projects
1999-2008

Location	Noordlaren, the Netherlands
Realized	1999
Client	Adri van der Sluis and Jet Visser
Team	Haiko Meijer, Alex van de Beld, Jeroen Boersma

The wooden barn contains all kinds of modern functions for everyday life. Its archetypical architecture fits into the rural context but, at the same time, its appearance is new and strange because of the articulated roof. The old shape has been blown up and transformed into something unexpected. It is made of re-used oak construction beams and western red cedar, all assembled by traditional construction methods.

I swear to submit to the following set of rules drawn up and confirmed by DogmA 01:

1. The design must be made specifically for the location.
   No pre-designed parts or details may be used.

2. The facade(s) must never be designed apart from the plan(s) or vice versa.

3. Drawings and models are hand-made. Architecture can be visualized by computer models, but computer programs do not generate architecture.

4. Materials are used as they are. Covering and colour coatings are forbidden.

5. Reference images and photomontages in the drawings are forbidden.

6. The building must not contain superficial or unnecessary constructions and ornaments.

7. Temporal and geographical alienation is forbidden.
   That is to say that the architecture takes place here and now.

8. Style designs are not acceptable.

9. All drawings must be made by the architect.

10. The architect must not be credited.

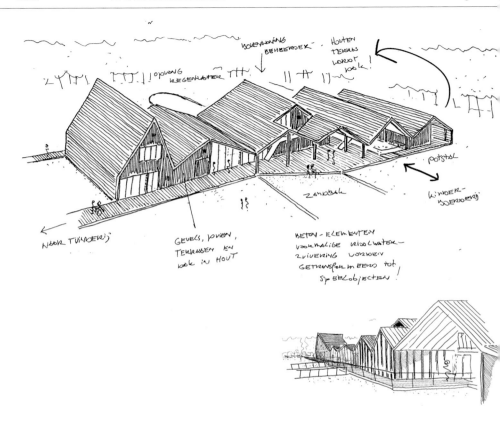

Location	Haren, the Netherlands
Realized	2003
Client	Stichting Ecologische Boerderij De Mikkelhorst
Team	Haiko Meijer, Alex van de Beld, Siert-Willem Helder, Berit Ann Roos, Martijn Woldring, Femke Pijnaker, Dirk Osinga

On two adjacent islands on the site of a former sewage plant, a complex programme of recreational (tea house, shop, educational space and children's farm) and care functions (caretaker's flat and office and work space for three different care institutions) has been realized. One island has been laid out as a market garden for the care institutions. The other, tree-ringed, island is laid out as a farm with the various functions arranged below a series of folded roofs. The different sections of the building are linked by a wooden front veranda. The variation in roof

width and pitch gives the impression of an informally evolved whole. The roof is the binding element holdin the different programme components together. These are in turn divided into two climatologically different groups: the 'house', containing the care institutions and (in two lofts) their offices and the caretaker's flat, and th 'stables' containing the farm activities. The below-roof space is particularly large above the 'stables' to allow for possible changes or extensions to the programme. Inside the building there are very few corridors, the ma spaces being connected by means of sliding doors. The farm is almost entirely built of (largely untreated) wood - not just the structure, roof, facades and frames, but th floors, walls, ceilings and doors as well.

–   *Yearbook Architecture in the Netherlands 2003-200 NAi Publishers, Rotterdam, p. 159.*

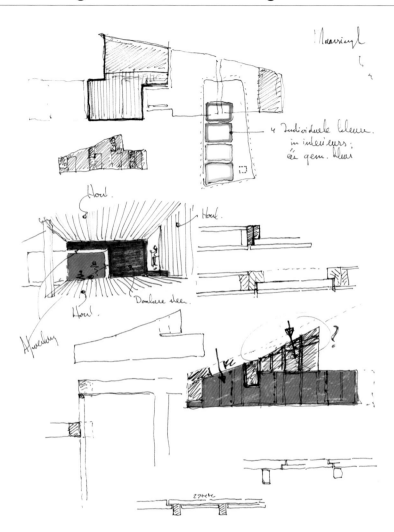

Location   Leeuwarden, the Netherlands
Realized   2005
Client   Bernhard Maarsingh and Irma van Steijn

Architect's explanation: inspired by the DogmA rules, a detached house was built in the Zuiderburen district of Leeuwarden. The design and all the details were made specially for this house. The facades follow logically from the plan and vice versa. The models for the house were handmade. The drawings of the house

contain only architectural information. Materials are used in accordance with their nature. The architecture of the house contains no ornaments or references to architectural movements. It is an architecture of the here and now. The house is an open book. The entire construction process was supervised by the architect. This is not an Onix house.

–   *Yearbook Architecture in the Netherlands 2005-2006* NAi Publishers, Rotterdam, p. 139.

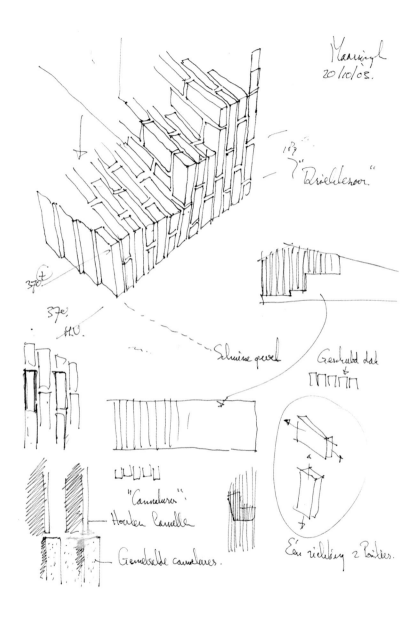

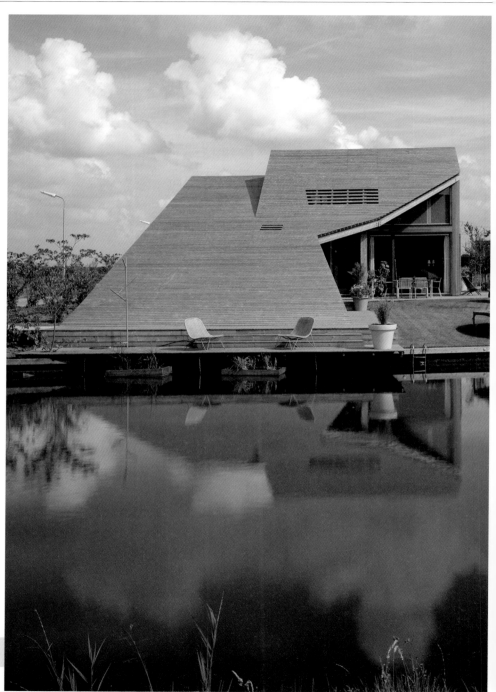

maNUfesto for an authentic experience of architecture:

1. walk around the building before entering it
2. draw the building
3. make your way through the building by wandering
4. visit the building by day and by night
5. make notes about your experiences
6. tell your memories to the building
7. set off from the building without leaving it
8. smell, feel, see, hear and taste the building
9. meet other people in the building
10. open up to someone else's experiences

Over a six-month period, Onix invited guests – from expert architecture critics to absolute laypeople – to stay in an unfinished apartment of the Exodus building. In return, the visitors noted down their experiences with neighbours, shops and public transport, representing a completely new form of architectural critique.

Program   housing, shops and parking at
                  Stadshagen shopping centre
Location   Zwolle, the Netherlands
Realized   2005
Client   ING Real Estate
Team   Haiko Meijer, Alex van de Beld, Jeroen
Boersma, René Harmanni, Femke Pijnaker, Jonathan
Woodroffe (S333), Gimill Mual (S333), Dagobert
Beagmens (S333), Allart Vogelzang, Martijn Woldring,
Buddy de Kleine, Siert-Willem Helder, Klaas Pieter
Lindeman, Johan Viswat (scale models)

The Exodus building is located in a suburban housing
area in the city of Zwolle. It contains an underground
car park that is cut open towards the new waterfront.
There are shops on the ground floor, above which are
80 varying types of apartments. As an intermediary
object, the goal of the building is to redefine architecture
between the global and the local, public and private,
transparency and isolation.

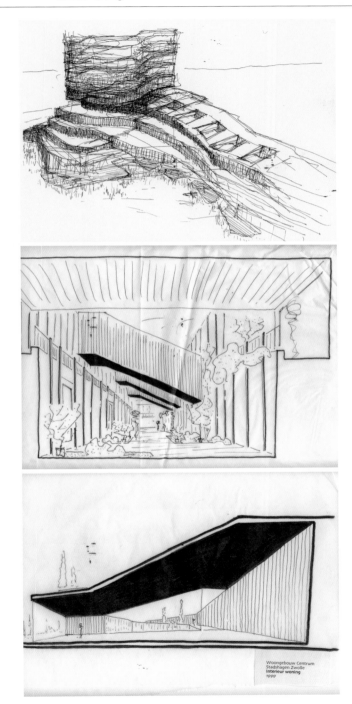

Woongebouw Centrum
Stadshagen Zwolle
Interieur woning
1999

Project	temporary building for an art assignment
Location	Bareveld, the Netherlands
Realized	2002
Client	Stichting 'Star and Arts', Stadskanaal
Team	Haiko Meijer, René Harmanni, Siert-Willem Helder, Allart Vogelzang, Berit Ann Roos, Buddy de Kleine, Alex van de Beld, Annemieke Meems, Alco Liest, Astrid Boelmans, Eefje van der Wielen, Martijn Woldring, Femke Pijnaker, with youngsters and farmers from Bareveld

Project	building nests
Realized	2005
Team	Alex van de Beld, Petter Haufman (N.O.D.), Peter de Kan, with Zizi and Yoyo, Tallinn and local students

Location	Almere, the Netherlands
Realized	2006
Client	NCB Projectrealisatie, Harderwijk
Team	Haiko Meijer, Siert-Willem Helder,
	René Harmanni, Klaas Pieter Lindeman

In the endless sea of houses that is Almere an exceptional housing scheme has been built. In a clear-felled 'room' in a poplar wood, stand 36 dwellings in ten separate volumes arranged around a shared space. All the dwellings have an outdoor area in the form of a large veranda on the south-west, that flows into a green bank. Car parking, entrance and storage have been placed at ground level up against this bank and underneath the house. The result is typologically a drive-in house, but given the focus on the natural surroundings and the large veranda the effect is more reminiscent of a chalet. Veranda and roof were designed as a single unit which strengthens the focus on the landscape.

Thanks to the architecture and the meticulous composition of the public space, several standard problems associated with low-rise have been resolved i one fell swoop: the car is tucked away beneath the hous and a natural distance has been created between private and public space, thereby removing the need for fences. The green area in-between really is the joint property of all residents. The already mature trees surrounding the site, the preponderance of timber in the construction and the orientation all conspire to strengthen the sense of privacy and of living in the middle of the forest.

–   *Yearbook Architecture in the Netherlands 2006-2007*
    NAi Publishers, Rotterdam, p. 86.

a non-contemporary pilgrimage in 10 paths

1.   NOWthentic
   Path 1 is each time a new road that ends in a mimesis of the authentic.

2.   scenius loci
   Path 2 is trodden together by local parties and outsiders.

3.   in between
   Path 3 seeks its way between object and environment.

4.   UNI space
   The individual Path 4 is accountable to the collective and public space.

5.   undecorated shed
   Path 5 leads to the moment when the naked primal type is abandoned.

6.   bush hammering
   On Path 6 improvisation will be predominant in the transitions and ruptures between the expected and the unexpected.

7.   non-contemporary
   On Path 7 time is taken to reflect on the making of sustainable decisions.

8.   unfamiliar familiarity
   From Path 8 convention is illuminated through emancipation.

9.   found footage
   The material is found on Path 9 that can take on a different meaning through a new application.

10.   uneXpected
    The exception to the rule is celebrated on Path 10, leading to sublime ecstasy.

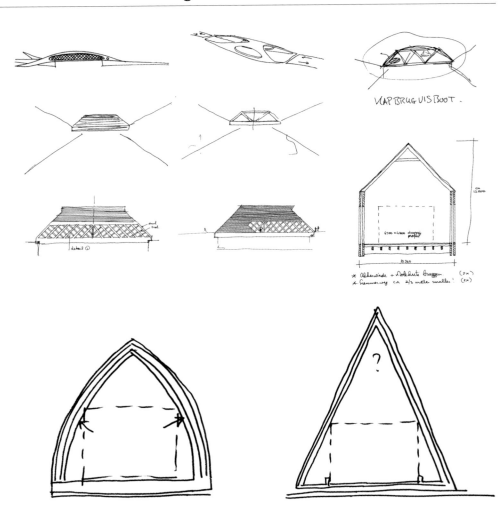

KAP BRUG VIS BOOT.

Location	A7 at Sneek, the Netherlands
Realized	2008
Client	Province of Friesland
Team	Haiko Meijer, Hans Achterbosch, Alex van de Beld, Erik-Jan Tabak, Emil Luning

This road bridge connects two districts of the city of Sneek, the Netherlands, on either side of the A7 motorway. It is realized in a responsible and sustainable way, and capitalizes on the latest innovations in wood construction. The contours call to mind the traditional cheese-cover farmhouses of Friesland. The constructic evokes reminiscences of the building expertise which is still abundantly present in the old city, whereas the wooden beams reflect the shipbuilding industry, with Sneek as the water recreation city par excellence in the North Netherlands.

Location	Lemmer, the Netherlands
Realized	2007
Client	private
Team	Haiko Meijer, Allart Vogelzang, Hep Beetsma, Fadi Alnajar

In response to the request to convert a traditional Frisia farmstead to a modern dwelling house, the assignment was translated into an architectonic concept of a house-in-the-roof. Elements with special aesthetic qualities, like the trusses and the large monumental roof, were retained. The house is seeking its own specific space in the area under the roof, looking for new locations for living, eating, working, and relaxing. The Searching House assigns new significance to the site, while still retaining its traditional farmstead character.

Alexander van Slobbe

Alexander van Slobbe

In 2003, Alexander van Slobbe (b. 1959) breathed a new lease
of life into his Orson + Bodil label for women, having sold his
successful menswear line, SO. The rationale was to free himself of
the commercial straitjacket of the prêt-à-porter fashion industry.
His Orson + Bodil collections are imbued with a smallness of scale
and experimentation within traditional craftsmanship. Van Slobbe
focuses emphatically on the intrinsic qualities of the garment. The
ensembles are sober and pure, distinguished by a subtle and highly
sophisticated exclusivity owing to their structure, the tactile qualities of
the materials, the manual workmanship and the physical experience
of form. The exploratory process of discovering the appropriate form
and structure involves using the technique of moulage, modelling
the garment on the actual mannequin. The handcrafted aspect is
manifest in detailing created using a 17th-century crochet technique
as well as in the employment of hand-printed textiles and felt. Van
Slobbe is highly conscientious in ensuring the entire production
process takes place in the Netherlands, in order to build a tradition
within Dutch fashion and to revive forgotten techniques. Van Slobbe's
long-standing collaboration with the oldest ceramics manufacturer in
the Netherlands, Royal Tichelaar Makkum, for which he has already
designed porcelain buttons and 'pearls', is the clearest example of this.

"I have been using handicraft techniques to position myself in the fashion world. When I graduated in the 1980s, it was the heyday of prêt-à-porter. Clothing was flat: completely frontally designed, as though the back, sides and interior were irrelevant. On the other hand, couture was more dead than alive and functioned above all for the creation of a perfume label. Handicrafts had been drastically cut down; you could still expect a handmade tear, but certainly not a hand-stitched hem. I started to work with moulage in reaction to both developments. It is a manual design technique that is precisely about the fullness, the three-dimensionality of the piece of clothing, because the fabric is draped around the model. The current popularity of craftsmanship has two causes: the quality of the craftsmanship has improved, and the quality standard has changed. Naturally leavened bread was always healthy but indigestible. Thanks to the development of the food industry, it is now healthy and tasty. If it was regarded as alternative in the past, it now stands for quality. While a hand-knitted jumper could not compete with design in the past, the situation today is completely the opposite. You can feel the force and the time that I have taken to knit this shawl specially for you.

More quality – even better, even more beautiful – has always been my principle. I do not expect to save the world with my handmade buttons and pure cashmere. What I am interested in is an emotion: something should feel, smell, fit nicely. That is how I work as well. Techniques and materials pass by at random and I select on the basis of emotion. The improvement is in the depth, not in the quantity.

This is not a new trend, but certainly after the present crisis the norm will change for good. The art of wanting less instead of consuming too much is how it will be. I find abstractions and emptiness incredibly interesting. If there's no need for a fastener or a pocket in a skirt, then I don't include them. My house has been bare for years. I don't want the burden of a whole service, but just four plates. Exactly the right number, but of superior quality."

Collections
2005-2009

Cotton braiding

Crochet

Crochet and embroidery

Crochet and embroidery

 Braiding and crochet embroidery

2006   Pearls from Makkum

Alexander van Slobbe and ceramics manufacturer Royal Tichelaar Makkum share the ambition
to reinvigorate the surviving traditional skills in the
Netherlands by means of boundary-breaking design.
Tichelaar had already produced porcelain buttons
for Van Slobbe, but their collaboration was crystal-
lized by the *Pearls from Makkum* project. In operation
since 1572, Royal Tichelaar is the oldest factory in
the Netherlands and is world-famous for its pottery
and porcelain. The firm has previously entered into
collaborations with designers such as Hella Jongerius,
Jurgen Bey, Marcel Wanders and Studio Job, in order
to extend the boundaries of traditional craftsmanship.

The *Pearls from Makkum* are fairly large porcelain
jewels that are modelled and decorated by hand.
Van Slobbe has created multifaceted, halved and
hand-painted variants as a complement to the classic spherical pearl. The pearls are available in several colours and decorative patterns. The pearls
are strung on a specially produced 100% silk cord.
Besides the complete necklaces produced in a limit
edition of 100, it is also possible to assemble a uniq
necklace using personally selected pearls.

2006   Orson + Bodil Perfume

Perfume is inextricably linked with the repertoire of a fashion designer. In a limited edition of 200 bottles, the perfume by Van Slobbe provides fresh evidence of his endeavours to create high-quality, sustainable and exclusive products. The perfume is 100% oil-based and contains no less than 20% perfume oil. The ingredients are aldehydes of lemon, raspberry, plum, cinnamon bark, laurel, mint, oakmoss, basil, white honey, tuberose absolute, rose absolute, lily of the valley, jasmine absolute, orris, geranium, bourbon, Moroccan artemisia, patchouli, Siamese benzoin, orange flower, ylang-ylang, amber, olibanum, heliotrope, sandalwood, civet and vanilla.

The crystal bottle has a hand-painted porcelain cap manufactured by Royal Tichelaar Makkum. Each bottle is numbered, and the number is registered together with the buyer's name upon purchase.

Porcelain pearl gilded with 18-carat gold

Printed by hand

Eighteenth-century Turkish
embroidery with gold thread

Laser-cut by hand

Eighteenth-century Turkish embroidery with gold thread

Cut, punched and
finished by hand

Porcelain button

Dyed by hand

Dyed by hand

Cut by hand on the
mannequin (moulage)

Dyed by hand

Crochet using strips of the same fabric as the garment

Crochet using strips of the same fabric as the garment

Semi-machined, modern *trapunto* (stuffed work)

Knitwork using strips of fabric

 Braiding and porcelain pearls

Porcelain pearls and buttons

Ribbon lacing combined with braiding in
the same fabric as the garment (tailoring)

Ribbon lacing combined with braiding in
the same fabric as the garment (decoration)

Ribbon lacing combined with braiding in
the same fabric as the garment (decoration)

Lining and exterior of skirt and jacket basted together by hand

 Dart also determines drapé of sleeve

Bodice basted by hand to V-neck

Strips of silk basted to front and back by hand

Organic hand-embroidered fabric of silk, silver, mohair and crystal

Four separate sheathes fitted into one another and basted by hand

 Two straight lengths with armhole and folds at neck and side seams

Collar attached by hand with laces and ribbon

Acknowledgements

Publication   This publication coincides with the travelling exhibition *Tangible Traces. Dutch Architecture and Design in the making*, curated by the Netherlands Architecture Institute.
This publication was made possible by financial support from the Netherlands Architecture Fund/HGIS Culture Fund, the Mondriaan Foundation, and the Netherlands Architecture Institute.

Compiled and edited by	Linda Vlassenrood, NAi
Essays by	Linda Vlassenrood / Mirjam van der Linden, Louise Schouwenberg / Joost Grootens, Roemer van Toorn, Blommers / Schumm
Design	Hansje van Halem
Image editing	Linda Vlassenrood, in cooperation with Hansje van Halem and Katja van der Sandt
Translation	Andrew May, Peter Mason (texts by Roemer van Toorn and Linda Vlassenrood / Mirjam van der Linden)
Lithography and printing	NPN Drukkers
Production	Caroline Gautier, NAi Publishers
Publisher	Eelco van Welie, NAi Publishers

NAi Publishers is an internationally orientated publisher specialized in developing, producing and distributing books on architecture, visual arts and related disciplines.
www.naipublishers.nl

Although every effort was made to find the copyright holders for the illustrations used, it has not been possible to trace them all. Interested parties are requested to contact NAi Publishers, Mauritsweg 23, 3012 JR Rotterdam, the Netherlands, info@naipublishers.nl

Available in North, South and Central America through D.A.P./Distributed Art Publishers Inc, 155 Sixth Avenue 2nd Floor, New York, NY 10013-1507, tel +1 212 627 1999, fax +1 212 627 9484, dap@dapinc.com

Available in the United Kingdom and Ireland through Art Data, 12 Bell Industrial Estate, 50 Cunnington Street, London W4 5HB, tel +44 208 747 1061, fax +44 208 742 2319, orders@artdata.co.uk

Printed and bound in the Netherlands
ISBN 978-90-5662-328-9

Exhibition

The travelling exhibition *Tangible Traces. Dutch Architecture and Design in the making* has been curated by the Netherlands Architecture Institute (NAI) and was possible with the support of the Netherlands Architecture Fund, Gispen International BV and Vitra. More information www.nai.nl

Commissioner	Ole Bouman
Curator	Linda Vlassenrood
Project Assistant	Stijn Kemper
Production	Karin Reinders
Exhibition Design	Studio Makkink & Bey
Execution	Landstra & de Vries
Graphic Design	Hansje van Halem
Illustrations	Yke Schotten
Coordination	
Travelling Exhibition	Fanny Smelik

Venues

- 7th International Architecture Biennial São Paulo, Brazil
  2 November 2007 - 15 December 2007
- Design Week Vienna, Austria
  4 October 2008 - 19 October 2008
- Business of Design Week Hong Kong, Hong Kong
  8 December 2008 - 21 December 2008
- Erasmushuis Jakarta, Indonesia
  9 February 2009 - 27 March 2009
- Museum of Modern Art, Arnhem, the Netherlands
  4 December 2009 - 28 February 2010

Linda Vlassenrood has worked as a curator at the Netherlands Architecture Institute (NAI) since 2000 and has been chief curator since 2008. She has curated a large number of exhibitions, including *Reality Machines. Mirroring the Everyday in Contemporary Dutch Architecture, Photography and Design* (2003) and *Tangible Traces. Dutch Architectecture and Design in the making* (2007), in which she combined several different disciplines. *Tangible Traces* was the Dutch contribution to the 7th São Paulo Architecture Biennial. She was also responsible for *Hybrid Landscapes*, the Dutch contribution to the Ninth Architecture Biennale in Venice. Other exhibitions that she has curated are *China Contemporary* (a joint initiative of the NAI, Museum Boijmans Van Beuningen and the Netherlands Photo Museum in 2006), and more recently the event *Shape our Country. Workshop for National Planning* (2008/2009).

Illustration credits

ANP Photo Xtra Lex van Lieshout ——————— 16/2

AP/Reporters ————————————————— 16/4

Nina Berman/Redux/Hollandse Hoogte ——— 19/3

Korrie Besems (Oostmahorn, Esonstad, 2006) — 12/1

Blommers / Schumm —— 196-207, 211-218, 227-230

Cermivelli ———————————————————— 12/2

Ben Cheung ————————————————— 49

Michel Claus ————————————————— 142

Cooper Hewitt, National Design Museum ——— 145

Peter Cox ——————————————————— 143

Peter Cuypers ————— 131, 132-136, 137, 138-139

Willem Franken

(thanks to architectenbureau K2) ——————— 15/5

Fabrice Gousset (courtesy Galerie Kreo) ——— 99

Frank Havermans ————————————— 33/2

Allard van der Hoek

(thanks to Joustra Reid Architecten) ————— 15/3

Leslie Holland ————————————————— 15/1

Jimmys Farm S1 26/05/2004 © BBC ———— 20/3

Rob de Jong SAPh ——— 166, 174-175, 182, 190-191

Jongeriuslab ————————————————— 85-98

Sabine Joosten/Hollandse Hoogte ————— 17/2

Leo van Kampen —————————————— 43

Peter de Kan ——— 167, 171, 180-181, 183, 188-189

Michael Kooren/Hollandse Hoogte ————— 12/4

Charles Kraft ————————————————— 16/3

Jannes Linders ———————————————— 140-141

Maarten van Loosbroek ————————————— 33/1

Marshall Astor Food Pornographer ——————— 19/4

Mcc d H —————————————————————— 20/1

Marc Mulders ——————————————————— 144

Jeroen Musch ————————————— 15/4, 104-105,
————————————— 127, 128, 129, 130, 184-185

Erica Overmeer ——————————————— 7/1, 7/4

Philippe Petit/PARISMATCH/

SCOOP/Hollandse Hoogte —————————— 20/5

Qiao-Da-Ye ————————————————— 19/2

Redwork ——————————————————— 19/5

Galerie Thaddeus Ropac ——————————— 19/6

Daria Scagliola & Stijn Brakkee (Soeters

Van Eldonk architecten, Sjoerd Soeters) ——— 12/3

Oliver Shuh (thanks to JDdVarchitecten/

Ex Interiors, Vreeswijk-Nieuwegein) ————— 15/2

Peter Stigter ————————— 219-226, 231-243

Roel van Tour ———————— 7/2, 7/3, 26, 54,
——————————— 57-81, 102, 149, 194

Carin Verbruggen.com

(thanks to Marlies Dekkers) —————————— 16/1

Marcel van der Vlugt ————— 108-109, 114-115

Dave Wadsworth ——————————————— 20/4

Wissing stedebouw en ruimtelijke vormgeving — 12/5

René de Wit —————————— 32, 34-35, 36-41,
————————————— 42, 44-45, 46-47, 48, 50-51

Mark van der Zouw/Hollandse Hoogte ——— 19/1